A Pictorial History of
INDIAN CINEMA

A Pictorial History of

INDIAN CINEMA

Firoze Rangoonwalla

HAMLYN
London · New York · Sydney · Toronto

To
ALI ASGHAR BAIG
Whose collaboration in this
book and my previous ones
has been invaluable.

Acknowledgments

We gratefully acknowledge the help of the following people and
concerns in providing some of the illustrations for this book:
Prem Sagar, Sagar Art International; B. Nagi Reddi, Vijaya Productions
(Madras); N. C. Sippy, Rupam Chitra; Tarachand Barjatya, Rajshri Pictures;
B. R. Chopra, B. R. Films; Mohan Segal, De Luxe Films; V. Shantaram,
Rajkamal Studios; Shyam Benegal, Sahyadri Films; Cyrus Tata, Bilmoria &
Lalji (Calcutta); Chhabra brothers, Chhabra Film Exchange; Bashir
Colombowala, Pushpa Pictures; Suresh Jindal, Devki Chitra; R. B. Mane,
Films Division; Anil Dharker, Film Finance Corporation; J. B. H. & Homi
Wadia, Wadia Bros. Productions; Kantilal Rathod, Akar Films; K. A. Abbas,
Naya Sansar; A. A. Nadiadwala, A. G. Films; I. A. Nadiadwala,
A. K. Movies; Shriram Bohra, Bohra Films; Manoj Kumar, V. I. P. International;
Raj Khosla, Raj Khosla Films; Basu Bhattacharya, Arohi Films; Rinky
Bhattacharya, Bimal Roy Productions; G. N. Lakshmipathy,
L. & N. Combines (Madras); M. Bhaktavatsala, Sharda Movies (Bangalore);
Dev Anand, Navketan International; Raj Kapoor, R. K. Films; Pramode
Chakravarty, Pramode Films; Shakti Samanta, Shakti Films; J. Om Prakash,
Filmyug; Ms. Neena, Filmistan; F. C. Mehra, Eagle Films; Atmaram,
Guru Dutt Films; the late D. C. Goel, Goel Cine Corporation; Mrinal Sen,
Mrinal Sen-Productions; Kidar Sharma, Ambitious Movies;
Hasmukh Solanki, Prafulla Studio; L. R. Trading Co. (Bombay).

Also of the following individuals for their co-operation:
Nemai Ghosh (photographer, Calcutta); Vijay Gupta (Calcutta);
B. Vishwanath Reddi (Madras); Mobin Ansari; Harish Mehra;
Abraham Thomas; Sanjit Narwekar and Bipin Bharucha.

endpapers Mrinal Sen's Hindi film *Mrigayaa*,
1976, with Mamta Shankar (left).
title page Aparna Das Gupta in *Samapti* by
Satyajit Ray.
half-title page A scene from *Dharam Veer*.

Published by
The Hamlyn Publishing Group Limited
London · New York · Sydney · Toronto
Astronaut House, Feltham, Middlesex, England

© Copyright The Hamlyn Publishing Group Limited 1979
ISBN 0 600 34909 8

Filmset in Great Britain by Photocomp, Birmingham
Printed in Hong Kong

Contents

Early Landmarks

The arrival of motion pictures in India was heralded first by this advertisement in *The Times of India* on 7 July 1897.

It may sound ridiculous to say that motion pictures in India began in the hotel and are still there, but both the past and the present give enough evidence of the fact.

The first-ever film to be screened in India was shown at the Watson's Hotel in Bombay, on 7 July 1896. It was the Lumiere Brothers' 'Cinematographe', which had brought the magical new device of showing the living moving pictures, advertised in *The Times of India* as 'the marvel of the century' and 'wonder of the world'. The items shown included *Arrival of a Train*, *The Sea Bath* and a curious little piece, *Ladies and Soldiers on Wheels*.

Now, after more than eight decades, the impression conveyed is more or less the same. The big, luxurious, air-conditioned cinemas rival the hotels in their gaudy decor, glass panelling and bizarre lighting. People come to the cinema not to see a creative work or a composite form of artistic expression, but to relax, enjoy themselves and vicariously experience whatever they have been missing just as their great-grandparents did in 1896.

The Lumiere's large stock of small films ran at Watson's and the Novelty Theatre to packed houses. The lowest 'gallery' admission charge was four annas and for the 'orchestra' it was two rupees; special enclosures were provided for ladies who came in 'pardah' and even music was added to the dumb show with a band led by a Mr. Seymour Dove. The programme ended on 15 August 1896, but the Indian audience had made it amply clear that they wanted more and more and so from 4 January 1897 there began a regular flood of imported movie shows at the Gaiety Theatre led by a Mr. Stewart's Vitugraph, trumpeted as 'the latest scientific invention' and again, with amazing originality, as 'the wonder of the world'. Mr. Stewart faced some unexpected competition from Signor Roberty, a self-styled American wizard showing live feats of necromancy and black art at the Tivoli, but black magic soon took a beating from black and white movie magic and the grand attraction in Bombay was *The Jubilee Procession* on the screen. As the blurb put it: 'to those who were unable to witness the great jubilee procession in U.K., an opportunity is offered at the Framjee Cowasjee Hall at Dhobi Talao'. At the end of the year the Tivoli itself offered 'the new improved Cinematograph' and with a 'Can Can Dance' in natural colours, too.

Several short films followed including *Mr. Gladstone's Funeral*, *Death of Nelson*, *Call on the London Fire Brigade* and *Scenes of the Greco-Turkish War* until some operators glanced nearer home and photographed *Our Indian Empire — Delhi, the Rome of Asia* and *Lucknow, Great Imambara Palace*. In 1898, Professor Anderson (with the able help of Mademoiselle Blanche) captured *A Train Arriving at Bombay Station* and *Poona Races '98* and included them in the Christmas revels of his show called Andersonoscopograph, which he claimed to have held earlier before Her Majesty the Queen Empress Victoria. At the same time in Calcutta, Professor Stevenson's ventures (as recorded in *Amrit Bazar Patrika*) included *A Dancing Scene from the Flower of Persia* and *A Panorama of Indian Scenes and Processions*.

The next step was for an enterprising Indian to make the first indigenous shorts. H.S. Bhatvadekar, who already had a projection outfit, imported a British camera and filmed two shorts: a specially staged bout of two wrestlers and a man training a monkey. Both were shown in the last two months of 1899. Foreign films were still imported, of course, on 1 January 1900, the Tivoli put up 25 imported pictures on Edison's Projecting Kinetoscope, including one with a misleading name *Fatima, an Indian Dance.* For all the films, the theatre provided music by a European lady. Another show had already tried to add sound to the picture itself. It was Professor Von Geyer's exhibition of Bettcini's 'Microphonograph', showing what were called 'living pictures, voices and speeches'. All these shows were adequately announced in *The Times* as well as commented upon in its 'Local and Provincial' column, the first signs of film criticism in the country. Bhatvadekar then acquired a Lumiere camera cum projector (still preserved) and made more shorts.

The second pioneering effort came from F.B. Thanawalla and his Grand Kinetoscope, covering *Splendid New Views of Bombay* and *Taboot Procession*, a Muslim ceremony. In 1901, came the third, from Hiralal Sen in Calcutta, whose Royal Bioscope produced extracts from seven popular Bengali plays of the time. In 1905, J.F. Madan and his Elphinstone Bioscope Company of Calcutta created the first semblance of an industry

An advertisement for Bengal's first silent feature film.

NEW TENT-MAIDAN

Elphinstone Bioscope.

TO-DAY

3 PERFORMANCES 3

at 6-15 p m. and 9-30 p. m

ELPHINSTONE PRESENTS   For the First Time in India.

"SATYAWADI RAJA

HARISCHANDRA

The Great Dramatic Success of the Indian Stage. Adapted for the screen from the famous drama of the same name and featuring.

THE EMOTIONAL STAR— MISS SAVARIA

and supported by the "Irving" of the Indian Stage

MR. HORMUSJEE TANTRA

and the Baliwala Victoria Theatrical Co. of Bombay.
Produced under the sole supervision of The Elphinstone Bioscope Co. of Calcutta.

SATYAWADI RAJA HARISCHANDRA

In 5 Reels—7,000 Feet Long

This play, which has had a most successful run on the Indian Stage for the last forty years. It is a play which pictures.
THE LIFE OF A HINDU KING
who, surrounded by all the grandeur and luxury that wealth could give, yet lived the life of nobility and purity, to whom falsehood and injustice were as strangers, and whose very virtues excited the wonder and the envy of the Gods above.

SATYAWADI RAJA HARISCHANDRA

AN ALL-ELPHINSTONE PHOTO-PLAY

Also in addition to the above film masterpiece a sensational and thrilling drama entitled.

"FOR THE SAKE OF HER CHILD" Produced by the "DANMARK FILM CO"

In Three Reels—4,000 Feet Long Will be screened for the first time in India

PUNDLIK-PUNDLIK

that Popular Hindu Drama. Almost half the Bombay Hindu population has seen it last week and we want the other half to do so before a change of programme takes place. Also see our

NEW SCREAMING COMICS.

Don't fail to come to-night and bring your friends.

CORONATION CINEMATOGRAPH.

SANDHURST ROAD, GIRGAUM.

An advertisement for *Pundalik,* India's first silent feature film.

D. G. Phalke

with a regular exhibition cum production set-up. Indian narrative films, with a length of 30 to 40 minutes, considered to be features by the standards of those days, now seemed feasible, since many such story films had already arrived in India from other countries.

The first attempt at making a dramatic film was made by R. G. Torney with the aid of N. G. Chitre when they made *Pundalik,* based on the life of a saint of Maharashtra. The idea sprouted from their amateur dramatic club and the raw film, camera and cameraman were brought from Bourne and Shepherd's Bombay branch. *Pundalik* was released on 18 May 1912 at Coronation Cinematograph, paired in a double programme with *A Dead Man's Child,* but its Indian nature, close to the people, soon made it the prominent fare on the bill. The film ran for two amazing weeks, with the advertisements and leaflets calling upon the whole Hindu population to come and see it. On 25 May, *The Times* reviewed *Pundalik* generously by saying: 'As a religious drama it has few equals. The programme is as good as it can be made'.

There were also a couple of other attempts such as *Savitri* by S. N. Patankar and friends and *An Episode from Ramayana* produced for Cinema de Luxe, before the arrival of the popularly accepted first feature, D. G. Phalke's *Raja Harishchandra,* which was released on 3 May 1913, a year after *Pundalik* and at the same theatre. It was accompanied by short items on the stage and screen to fill the bill, being a four-reeler of 3700 feet. Its first run extended a little over three weeks, soon followed by a re-run at another theatre.

Phalke's unquestioned pioneering and fathering of the Indian feature film lie in the fact that the film was a wholly Indian venture or *Swadeshi* as he preferred to call it, in keeping with the patriotic spirit of the times.

Phalke, his family and film unit had struggled very hard to accomplish it, after his own visit to London to see, study and obtain equipment. And then, while his contemporaries gave up, Phalke continued to produce and thus laid the foundation of an industry, though he had to pass through the same ordeal again during the first World War despite having completed three films.

Phalke's own prolific writings in Marathi give us an idea of the hurdles he had to cross. He admits that he was first inspired by the film *Life of Christ* and started conceiving films with mythological gods as the characters. To get both the technical knowledge and material, he made a trip to London by mortgaging his insurance policy. As a newcomer to the city, he went to the office of the Bioscope Cine Weekly and met its editor Mr. Cabourne, who helped him in buying the right gadgets and also introduced him to pioneer Cecil Hepworth whose studio work Phalke could observe. But all this did not smooth his finance problems in India and he had to make a small trick shot film, *Growth of a Plant*, to prove his point. Among other problems, there was the prickly one of getting women for the female roles. The infant cinema must have been so much a suspect then, that even women of easy virtue were difficult to convince. Finally, Phalke had to ask one of the stage boys, Salunke, to put on saree, blouse and padding to play Queen Taramati to D. D. Dabke's King Harishchandra. For the royal son's role, Phalke picked his own son Bhalchandra. *Raja Harishchandra* proved a sumptuous hit.

In the same year, Phalke turned out *Mohini Bhasmasur* and even some short documentary films. Now, Phalke had two actual women to play the roles and the number jumped to four in his *Satyawan Savitri* which came in mid-1914. To get more printing machines, Phalke paid another visit to London and took along his three films. Mr. Cabourne helped to arrange a trade show and the *Bioscope Weekly* gave some rave advance notes. Most of the British papers were full of praise for Phalke's pictures, both for their content and technique and he was even asked to make films in Britain, but declined.

However, all this made little difference when he returned to India. War had broken out and finances dried up, especially for ventures which relied on imported material. After another long spell of suffering and

The bathing scene from *Raja Harishchandra* with D. D. Dabke in the title role and Salunke as Taramiti.

13

D. Bilimoria was a popular hero in both silent films and the early talkies.

An advertisement for *Shakuntala*.

sacrifice, Phalke came up in 1917 with a big hit *Lanka Dahan* (Lanka Aflame) and the whole scene changed again. Now he sought shelter in a partnership and the Hindustan Cinema Film Company was formed at Nasik. The first two films under the new banner were the immensely successful *Krishna Janma* (Birth of Shri Krishna) and *Kalia Mardan* (Childhood of Shri Krishna) in 1918 and 1919, both featuring his daughter Mandakini as little Krishna. She soon became a child star herself and won gold medals.

Phalke had indeed set the industry's ball rolling. A little before his fourth film, J. F. Madan in Calcutta came up with Bengal's first silent feature *Satyawadi Raja Harishchandra*, with an amazing length of 7000 feet. Miss Savaria and Homi Tantra of the Baliwala and Victoria Theatre companies acted in it, and it was screened in Bombay, in a tent cinema, soon after *Lanka Dahan*. From the South, the first effort, though a feeble one, which emerged in 1919, was Nataraj Mudaliar's *Keechaka Vadham* made in Madras. It was a tale from Mahabharata about the demon Keechaka's destruction. *The Mail* of Madras reviewed it favourably saying: 'it has been produced with great care and is drawing crowded houses'. In Bombay, Patankar Friends made *Exile of Shri Rama* the first serial in four parts and Suchet Singh brought the first non-Indian actress, Dorothy Kingdom from the U.S.A., to play in his *Shakuntala*.

From 1917, there followed a period of 15 years when silent films held sway and some 1280 were made in different genres. The next big development was the evolution of the talking picture. In India, the talkie did not immediately supercede the silent film. On the contrary, 200 silents were made in the first talkie year. But the sound film did replace the silent film within a couple of years.

Once again, the early history of talkies covered short items and a variety of attempts to make the moving pictures talk and also sing. The imported films in the late 1920s provided a tempting model but the machines and know-how were missing. In late 1928, Bombay's Capitol Cinema of the pioneering exhibitors Sidhwas showed some British talkies containing several shorts. The first Indian venture was a talkie pro-

gramme shown in September 1930 at the Krishna Cinema. There were two synchronised pictures, one of a Khadi exhibition with Mahatma Gandhi, C. F. Andrews and others appearing and speaking and the second a dance by that era's top star Sulochna taken from a silent film, *Madhuri*, and linked with music. Then, Madan Theatres and Krishna Film Co. prepared talkie shorts in 1931 containing songs, dances, skits, speeches and even lectures.

These two along with Imperial Film Co. were in a heated race to complete a talkie feature film. Imperial won the race with *Alam Ara* (Light of the world), released at Bombay's Majestic Cinema on 14 March 1931. Produced by Ardeshir Irani, who had already made dozens of silent films, it spoke a simple language which was a mix between Sanskrit-based Hindi and Persian-based Urdu. And it also presented seven catchy songs, which indeed caught on so well that they still can be heard today.

Alam Ara was a fantasy based on a popular drama and featured Zubeida, Master Vithal, Prithviraj Kapoor and W. M. Khan. The sound recording, done on the Tanar single-system (sound recorded with image), was handled by Wilford Demming jointly with Irani. The film was 10,000 feet long and was the expected incredible success. Soon after, indeed in the same year, there came twenty-two films in Hindi, three in Bengali (made at Calcutta), one in Tamil and one in Telugu (both made in Bombay).

Various other 'firsts' also began to be claimed, including the first film in an English version (Imperial's *Nurjehan* directed by Ezra Mir) and also the initial attempts in other Indian languages and even in Persian. The first attempt in colour was made by Madan Theatres in 1932 by getting their film *Bilwamangal* processed abroad. In the following year, Prabhat's *Sairandhri* was shot on a colour process and taken to Germany for prints. But technically both failed to make the grade. The first wholly Indian colour attempt was accomplished by Ardeshir Irani's *Kisan Kanya* in 1937, followed in the next year by *Mother India* both done on Cinecolor. Regular colour came much later in the 1950s with Mehboob's *Aan*, Sohrab Modi's *Jhansi Ki Rani*, Ambalal Patel's *Pamposh* and V. Shantaram's *Jhanak Jhanak Payal Baaje*.

Today, when every other film has some new technical finesse, is in colour, or in 70 mm, it is only proper to remember the efforts of those who laid the roots, with their sweat and often tears.

above left
A production still from *Pandava Nirvana*, a typical mythological silent from the South which was made in 1930.

above
Magic Box was an early talkie which was also produced in the South.

A scene from *Alam Ara* showing Jilloobai and Master Vithal as mother and son.

Myths
and Melodrama

The first Indian feature films were mythological epics and they are still filmed today. Their influence has trespassed into other genres, too, in thinly disguised forms.

The myth has a venerable cultural-religious tradition and the Indian mind has a strong attachment to it. Gods and goddesses are frantically, and in some places fanatically, worshipped. Myths about them are repeated from mouth to mouth. Lending further power to the myths' impact are the fable-like narratives and their morals. People of other communities also respect them out of tradition as well as having their own myths to suckle.

If it was *Raja Harishchandra* in 1913, it is *Jai Santoshi Maa* in 1975. If Taramati suffered great ordeals and injustices, her modern counterpart Satyavati goes through the worse, with a brand new goddess to rescue her with miracles. The great success of *Jai Santoshi Maa* all over India speaks volumes for the mental make-up of the present film audience and, more than that, for the power of Indian Cinema in resurrecting a little-known provincial goddess to a level where new temples for her have sprung up in all corners of the country.

Faith in divine deities as miracle workers plus a craving for magic solutions to the various problems of life lie behind the weakness for the mythological epic and its sister genre, the devotional. The former is a structure based on the mythical figures themselves, while the latter is about their devotees, usually fictional and from any period, who call for their appearance which is occasionally granted accompanied by miracles. The popularity of such films in the early silent days or just after the talkie's arrival could be understood, since cinema and its trick shots could add a new edge to the age-old tales, then popular on the stage. But since they have continued to hold sway, it shows up a fundamental weakness in people.

Among the most popular myths have been those from the epics Ramayana and Mahabharata and the countless tales connected with Lord Krishna from his childhood onwards. The ideal characters of Ramayana, as interpreted by Valmiki and Tulsidas, have provided an endless source of films showing good fighting and destroying evil in its worst forms. They have also justified the qualities of duty, sacrifice, chastity, tolerance et al, being virtues as practised by a vast majority of people, whether voluntarily or enforced by circumstances.

By and large, these themes have been treated in a crude, melodramatic, pseudo-devout fashion. The sufferings drive people to the extreme of tears, while on the other hand, the monkey-God Hanumaan becomes a figure of fun for the children in the audience. A keen cinema student once raised the rather disturbing point that since the goddesses and other revered females are dressed as temptingly as actresses in other films, the dilemma is whether or not to view them carnally.

The epics have now been drained of all their cinema-worthy episodes and have also been repeated ad infinitum. It was Debaki Bose's *Seeta* in 1934 which treated the theme in a different artistic way and became the first to be sent to an international festival — the Venice Cinematograph

The veteran actor V. Shantaram (centre) made his film debut in the 1921 silent mythological *Surekha Haran*. At that time acting was still considered a dubious profession for women and so V. Pagnis (right) played the heroine.

Lament of Gandhari, a 1931 silent mythological film from the South.

overleaf
V. Shantaram (left) as King Dushyanta and Sandhya as Shakuntala in a temple scene from *Stree*.

Saraswati Sabatham was a Tamil mythological film which starred Shivaji Ganeshan and Savitri.

Exhibition. Later, when the Hindi cinema was at its peak in the early 1940s the Ramayana epics were portrayed in some very fine film versions in Vijay Bhatt's *Bharat Milap* followed by the great hit *Ram Rajya*, which had a glow of philosophy and myth culture. However, most other films have been mechanical versions of the different episodes or several of them strung together. Bhatt himself tried a remake of *Ram Rajya* in the 1970s, but it turned out a shallow film. Mythologicals have been in the wrong hands mostly. Satyajit Ray toyed with the idea of making *Mahabharata* for many years.

The epics have been very common in the four South Indian language films. Hundreds of them can be found in Tamil and Telugu, though nearly all in the same vein of miracle-mongering and religion-peddling. Only in recent times have some experiments been made such as Bapu's *Seetha Kalyanam* which was treated in a ballad-like fashion. The South's mass-market films, including some Madras-made Hindi films, have made an interesting extension, especially of Ramayana, to other classes of films set in the present. Names of the divine people are often given as an implicit label to characters, the most popular being Radha, Krishna, Seeta, Rama and their other derivative names. But sometimes direct parallels of plots are drawn with clear allusions. For example, a recent film *Jeevan Jyoti* was almost Ramayana in a modern setting.

The tragedy of Seeta's exile by Rama and her rearing of her two sons in the forest has been applied in film after film, like a long shadow of Seeta falling on the screen heroines. Some films have also covered illegitimate children in it. In Muslim stories it has taken the form of an innocent woman ostracised as her chastity is doubted in films like *Zeenat* and *Shama*. Krishna's various legends in relation to Radha, Subhadra, Draupadi, apart from his consorts like Rukmini and Satyabhama, his killing of demons, his treatment of loving devotees and his escapades as a child have been seen in innumerable film versions. Still, the most remarkable, apart from Phalke's silent hits, were *Shyam Sunder* (1932) and Prabhat's *Gopal Krishna* (1938). The trend is still continuing with a new version made in 1978-79, with teen stars Zarina Wahab and Sachin.

Devotionals, though fewer, are equally popular and have led to an absurd blending in recent times of the modern day devotees physically mixing with the deities who come down to earth. An example is *Sampoorna Sant Darshanam* which films a tour of 1001 holy shrines and then virtually pits the gods-goddesses against male-female saints for the

The little devotee Prahlada stands before Lord Vishnu and his consort in *Bhakta Prahlada*, 1959.

Kalidasa's famous drama-poem *Shakuntala* was filmed in 1943 by V. Shantaram with Jayshree as Shakuntala and Chandramohan as Dushyanta.

sake of a modern worshipper. A parallel derivation is of the Muslim devotional, for example *Niaz Aur Namaz* or *Mere Gharib Nawaz*, where wish-fulfilling devout tales are told with an accent on rituals and beliefs.

A similar genre is folklore or legend about holy men and women, kings and queens, even outlaws and dacoits. These are often region-bound, like the tales from Gujarat and Saurashtra. There are also the stories of legendary love pairs, who lived and died for love. As some of these have a literary-cultural basis they have been promoted, at times even with the aid of state governments, as specimens of provincial heritage. *Heer Ranjah*, *Sohni Mahiwal*, *Mirza Sahiban* and *Dhola Maru* have been the romantic pairs popularised through the screen. Similar has been the case

opposite top
Sachin and Zarina Wahab, teen stars, play Krishna and Radha in *Gopal Krishna*.

opposite bottom
A scene from *Kondura*.

above
Sulakshana Pandit as the beautiful princess and Feroz Khan as the humble peasant in *Gule Bakavali*.

bottom left
The legendary love pair *Shirin Farhad* in a 1945 film of that name with Jayant and Ragini as the lovers.

Fearless Nadia courageously defeated wrongdoers in a series of films in the 1930s. Here she is triumphing over Sayani in Wadia Brothers' *Lutaru Lalna*, 1938.

Wrestler-actor Dara Singh here plays Lord Hanumaan in the popular mythological *Bajrangbali*.

with tales from classical sources, like *Mrichcha Katika* (Toy Cart), filmed as *Vasantsena*. In its silent version, the leading political and social figure Kamladevi Chattopadhyaya appeared in the cast.

Producers not willing to tax their brains even that far took easy recourse in the countless fantasies, costume and stunt pictures. This gave them a free form to operate in, though some like the Wadia Brothers, J. B. H. and Homi, injected a nationalist spirit, within the outer garb of masked amazons or daredevils winning back the Ruritanian kingdoms from those who had usurped them. The most popular such figure in the early talkie era was 'Fearless' Nadia wearing a mask and doing impossible feats in a series of films such as *Hunterwali* and *Hurricane Hansa*. Producers like Vijay Bhatt had another kind of thrillers going — *Passing Show* and *Hero No. 1*. They were of course broadly modelled on the lines of American serials and provided a regular diet for the lower classes. The stunts seemed to bring out the conflicts of the underprivileged classes and provide them relief giving images, for example robbing the rich and powerful to help the poor. In recent years, their heroes have taken various forms from Tarzan (known as Zimbo) to musclemen played by the popular wrestler Dara Singh.

Paramount Movietone of Kikubhai Desai churned out a number of fantasy and magic films in the 1930s, soon copied by others. Today his heirs Subhash and Manmohan Desai have raised this genre to the opulent level of grand, multistar films in colour and wide screen, a good example being *Dharam Veer*, while they also use the same elements in modern-day tales such as *Amar Akbar Anthony*, *Chacha Bhatija* and *Parvarish*. The pure fantasy itself has been rare, but its more popular forms like *Alibaba, Aladdin, Sindbad The Sailor, Thief of Baghdad* etc. have been made by the dozen. The costume and fantasy films are often given a muslim base to act as a countering influence and a way of catering to that section of the big Indian audience. However, the crowning glory of costume pictures was provided by Gemini Studios of South India invading the Hindi market with *Chandralekha*, a massive spectacular made in 1948.

By and large, all the non-myth genres have functioned as mythological byproducts, existing in a supernatural miracle world and promoting old-world beliefs and superstitions. In the innocent decades of Indian

Mahipal and Meena Kumari in *Aladdin and his Wonderful Lamp*.

Cinema, they looked humble and enjoyable, but today they have taken a lavish but hideous and concocted form. There was a joke about the old fantasies that, if the hero gave any trouble during the shooting, a quick twist of the script would turn him into a parrot, so that he would be needed only in the last scene. Now, the hero has turned everyone around him into parrots, who repeat whatever he says.

The drum dance from *Chandralekha*, a huge popular success produced in 1948.

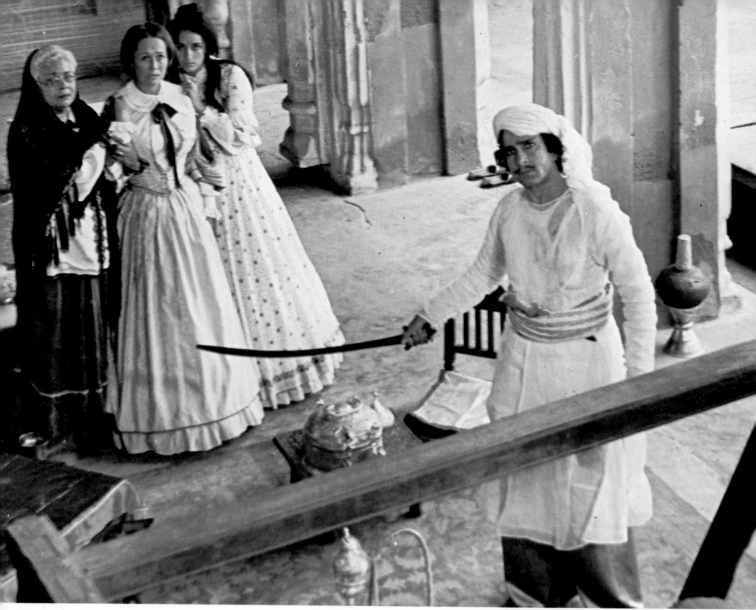

above
Junoon, directed by Shyam Benegal,
tells of a Pathan's love for a British girl
in the days of the Indian Mutiny. It
starred and was produced by Shashi
Kapoor who is seen here with (left to
right) Ismat Chugtai, Jennifer Kendal
and Nafeesa Ali.

right
War provides a backdrop for *Achanak*,
a drama of a soldier accused of
murdering his wife who eventually goes
to the gallows. It was produced by
N. C. Sippy.

opposite
Neetu Singh in a scene from the
costume drama, *Dharam Veer*.

The Historical Films

Mehtab as the famed warrior queen the Rani of Jhansi in *Jhansi Ki Rani*, 1953.

opposite top
Sohrab Modi's grand historical epic *Pukar*, 1939, about the Mughal King Jahangir.

opposite bottom
Sikander (Alexander), 1941, related the story of the Greek king's attempted invasion of India and his clash with the Indian ruler Porus. Prithviraj (centre) played Alexander.

overleaf top and opposite
Two scenes from *Mrig Trishna* which was inspired by the Japanese film *Ugetsu Monogatari*.

overleaf bottom
Siddhartha was set in the days of Buddha and starred Shashi Kapoor and Simi.

Next to the myth comes history and its related types: biographies of well-known saints and other great people, historical legends, films with wars as a background and the sagas of patriots and freedom fighters. Being non-fictional, they are supposed to be based on the truth, but the Indian Cinema has mostly acted under the presumption that they need not be strictly factual.

In the early silent years, the historical film was a handy visual device for showing grandeur through palaces, processions, battles, etc., since language was no barrier. Another motivation was to show the heroic quality of kings like Shivaji, whose exploits against the Mughals had a strong nationalist impact too. V. Shantaram tried to extend this to the prevailing British rule, through an outstanding silent film *Udaykal*, also titled as *Flag of Freedom*. But the political censorship of the day came down heavily on it so *Flag of Freedom* became *Thunder of the Hills* and a scene showing warriors hoisting a flag was one of several which were cut. Another episode, *Kalyan Khajina* (Treasures of Kalyan) where Shivaji honourably protects a woman belonging to the Mughal enemy camp, produced by Baburao Painter, gained wide popularity. Tales of valour from Rajasthan were also tried by Painter; one on queen Padmini called *Beauty of Rajasthan* or *Siege of Chitor* in its alternate English title was of high enough quality to win a certificate from the Wembley Exhibition and praises from the London press in 1924.

In the talkie period, more than anyone else it was Sohrab Modi who set the tradition for grand historicals. Although his early ones were not very authentic they were created in the fashion of dramatic anecdotes and romanticised legend so that the films: *Pukar*, *Sikander* and *Prithvi Vallabh* were a massive success. But when Modi tried a genuine history of the life of the queen of Jhansi the audiences were lukewarm. *Jhansi Ki Rani* (Tiger and the Flame) was an ambitious venture, the first in Technicolor to be shot in India with Ernest Haller coming over to do the lensing as well as other technicians and equipment brought over specially. Despite all its spectacle, it proved a giant flop. In his later film *Mirza Ghalib*, on the life of the famed Urdu poet of Bahadurshah Zafar's time, Modi again took recourse to 'drama', against which protests and objections were raised from the expected sources. The clash between history and fiction continued.

In recent times, Satyajit Ray brought about a remarkable combination of both in *Shatranj Ke Khiladi* based on Premchand's *Chess Players*. He expanded on the short story by etching the characters of General Outram (Richard Attenborough) and Wajid Ali Shah of Oudh (Amjad Khan), while the two chess-playing nawabs became a replica of their times and the people's attitude to life. The line between personal and political chess became thinner and thinner.

Straight biographical pictures have also been tried, though almost invariably possessing some fictional additions and some elements common to the popular cinema, especially songs and romantic interest. *Dr. Kotnis Ki Amar Kahani*, especially done in English as *Journey of Dr. Kotnis* was made by V. Shantaram as a worthwhile tribute to the self-

sacrificing doctor who gave his life in war-ravaged China while serving in a Congress medical mission and also taking a Chinese wife. Still, songs and other entertaining material could not be avoided. Shantaram also made films on Marathi poets, Honaji in *Amar Bhoopali* and Ramjoshi in a Hindi-Marathi film of that name. But the most unexpected was a screen biography of the screen idol K. L. Saigal, whose haunting voice has made him legendary. Called *Amar Saigal* (*Immortal Singer*), it was made/compiled by New Theatres of Calcutta where Saigal had given his best work.

Under Prabhat Film Co. of Poona, Gajanan Jagirdar directed and acted in *Ramshastri* based on the life of that unflinching judge from Maratha history. Yet, the best work in this genre has been done by Bengal, which has made surprisingly serious screen versions on the lives of various prominent personalities, among them Netaji Subhas Chandra Bose, Vidyasagar, Bhagini Nivedita, Raja Ram Mohan, Khudiram (the rebel) as well as spirited patriotic films on the freedom struggle two of which are

top
V. Shantaram and his actual wife Jayshree in the biography *Dr. Kotnis Ki Amar Kahani* which was made in 1946.

above
The biographical film *Ramjoshi* about the famous poet.

right
Ramshastri was about the great Maratha judge who accuses the Peshwa of murder and starred and was directed by Gajanan Jagirdar.

32

above
Arundhati Devi in the title role of
Bhagini Nivedita, a biography made in
1961.

left
A still from *Mirza Ghalib*, a biography
of the famous Urdu poet, with Bharat
Bhushan and Suraiya as his beloved.

Bhuli Nai and *42*. It is only attachment to one's region and its great souls
that can lead to the making of such attempts, which are usually
considered box-office poison.

In Hindi and Punjabi, the life of Bhagat Singh and other young martyrs
have been filmed in many versions, some remarkable and some mediocre,
right until the present. Tamil Nadu has made films on its heroes, for
example *Veer Pandya Kattabomman*. Semi-fictional films have also
adopted an inspiring background or personality to launch their plots:
Pahela Aadmi (about Subhas Bose), *Anandmath* on the freedom fight put
up by a cult of militant sadhus, *Andolan* on the freedom struggle itself
and *Sabyasachi* based on Sarat Chandra's novel which was banned before
India's Independence. But the subject has also been given a box-office
slant in many films where patriotism becomes a handy slogan and the
hero a cardboard martyr. Such films however have proved the biggest
hits with the public, like Filmistan's *Shaheed* (Martyr).

Though India has not really undergone the rigours of long-term wars,
some films have been made taking it as a focal point. It was mostly a case
of war being an excuse for a melodramatic plot with some martial songs
added and some news-reel footage (often non-Indian) used for 'atmos-
phere'. Though Indian producers and directors saw some of the finest
war films emerging from other countries, they neither had the resources
nor the intentions to take up a film about war itself. Only in recent years
have some films about some aspect of war been made, like *Haqeeqat* and

33

above
Tamil actor Shivaji Ganeshan in the
patriotic film *Veer Pandya
Kattabomman*, 1959.

above right
K. Asif's *Mughal-e-Azam* about
Anarkali, a court dancer, was a massive
success.

opposite top left
Kranti was one of the costliest films of
1979 and was set in the days of the
Indian mutiny. Manoj Kumar, its
director, and Hema Malini were two of
its many stars.

opposite top right
Sant Dynaneshwar is a typical saint
story featuring Shahu Modak as the
simple saint first ostracised then revered
for his humanist teachings.

opposite bottom
A scene from the devotional film
Bhakticha Mala.

Hindustan Ki Kasam. But there have also been light romances where the
hero joins the army after frustration in love.

While both remote and recent history have suffered, the pseudo or
semi-historical legends have flourished and yielded successful films
again and again. The most prominent case is of Anarkali, the poor dancer
in emperor Akbar's court who dares to love and be loved by the rich
'Prince Charming'. Anarkali's woes have found echoes in many versions,
all studded with songs and dances, including K. Asif's extravaganza
Mughal-e-Azam, with all its visual splendour and special highlights such
as the glass palace with a thousand reflections. So tenuous must be the
historical source that Anarkali has met different fates at the end of
different films, one of being buried alive and another of being set free
secretly by Akbar. One of the latest on the subject shows Anarkali's
daughter growing up and coming to accuse her royal father, who was by
then settled happily with Nurjehan.

Greatly different from these are the purely devotional films, narrating
the actual life and preaching of different saints including Meerabai,
Tulsidas, Surdas, Shankaracharya, Chaitanya, Narsinh Mehta,
Vidyapati, Kabir, Joidev or Avvaiyar (from South). The life of Buddha
has been a favourite from the early days and was made memorable by
Himansu Rai as the silent film *Light of Asia*, in 1925-26. A courageous
coproduction with Germany, the film took Indian cinema into the world
arena, even if only for a short while. It was drawn from Edwin Arnold's
poetic work, the verses being used as the sub-titles on the cards. In recent
years, Conrad Rooks has made *Siddhartha* from Hesse's novel based on
that period with Indian artistes Shashi Kapoor and Simi.

But stories of provincial and intimately known saints have proved a
far far bigger success. This trend began in Maharashtra with the filming
of the lives of locally-known saints. Their devotion, suffering and
teaching needed a wider exposure, however. With *Sant Tukaram*
becoming a great success in all communities, the path was paved for
other similar films such as *Sant Dnyaneshwar*. The great popularity of

these films may be because the local saints appear more trustworthy than the gods of mythology, though the former are supposed to be incarnations of the latter. Moreover, the religion which the saints preached was intimate and uncomplicated, based on humanist goals rather than rituals. No wonder that the saints on the screen are loved and worshipped and that the actors playing them have the not-so-deserving honour of feet-touching obeisance and their photos and posters being garlanded in the smallest of towns and villages.

Times are Modern, Traditions Old

opposite
A late silent film *All for Love* starred Jairaj in one of his earliest roles, here seen with screen actress Madhuri. Jairaj has appeared in films for 50 years.

England Returned

'Social' is a typical coinage of Indian Cinema to describe a film set in the present. So all films whose characters wear modern dress and live amidst twentieth century developments are socials, even though they may be anti-social in their content and impact and quite a few decades old in their concept. The young cinema is not so young and the modern cinema is not so modern. Traditions die hard in the country and harder in films.

ROMANCE

The commonest among the socials are the romances or love affairs, usually opposed and forbidden till the last by the parents, when the lovers either marry and sing happily again or die to the accompaniment of a sad background song, at times sung by the dying couple themselves. It seems that seeking a woman's love and staking everything to attain it, form the most important life-goal of the adult male. Various ruses and devices are tried to make the experience as pleasurable as possible for the audience. This has continued down to today with the 'young love' hits *Bobby* and *Ankhiyon Ke Jharonkhon Se*.

In fact, this craze for love and wooing arises from the long-standing social conditions, whereby any free mixing between the two sexes is taboo and customs such as dating are vehemently suppressed. Love after marriage and a little courtship, conditional on an engagement ceremony, are the guidelines laid down from generation to generation. So those who have missed and those who are missing a more lax lifestyle get it from the screen, through the inglorious sight of the hero chasing the girl, singing and dancing, making various romantic overtures to her and then lavishing all his energies to take her from the hands of the father or rival lover. Being alone with a woman is one of the most potent dream formulas of Indian Cinema and directors as well as writers keep whipping their brains to devise different ways of bringing it about.

Love stories thus form a large chunk of the socials. In the early days, both of silent and talkie, it was done with legendary love pairs of whom Laila Majnu and Shirin Farhad are a good example. Then the focus was shifted to modern times. In the silents, the trend was started by Bengal's D. G. (Dhiren Ganguli) who began with a satire *England Returned* in 1921 and made two mischievous little films: *Lady Teacher* and *Marriage Tonic*. Directors in other regions followed up with films like *Society Scoundrel* and *Handsome Blackguard*. (Silent films then had their first titles in English to draw the elite audience accustomed to imported films.)

In the talkies, the pioneers were J. F. Madan of Madan Theatres who filmed stageplays of his own theatrical company and Chandulal Shah of Ranjit who made *Miss 1933* with his favourite star, Gohar. All this continued till *Devdas* came and swept away everything. It was the ultimate in love, based on Sarat Chandra's story, made by New Theatres and directed by P. C. Barua, with himself playing Devdas in the Bengali version and Saigal playing Devdas in the Hindi one. The essence of *Devdas* is love denied by class differences, so that the man drifts to ruin with wine and woman while the beloved becomes the housewife of a rich widower with children of the same age as their step-mother. In a much

The top singer-actor K. L. Saigal and Jamuna as the girl he cannot marry in *Devdas*, 1935, one of the most influential films of Indian Cinema.

This re-make of *Devdas* in 1955 starred Dilip Kumar as the tragic hero with Motilal as his happy-go-lucky friend.

adored ending, Devdas makes a long cart journey in the last stage of his life, to die at Parvati's doorstep.

The tragedy of *Devdas* was meant to provoke protest against the sheer cruelty of the situation taken so casually for granted by the elders and the society of the time. The prostitute who entertains Devdas and emancipates herself with his love without achieving it was an equally pathetic creature crying out for social change. But the film also let off the contrary currents, of gloom, frustration as a credo and fatalism. To manifest a different belief and also as a faint signal of inter-producer conflict, V. Shantaram under the Prabhat banner brought out *Aadmi*. Its English title *Life Is For Living* speaks for itself. A policeman failing to rehabilitate a prostitute whom he dearly loves is asked to overcome his obsession and concentrate upon his profession. This film too succeeded. But the more popular example was set by *Devdas*. And its long shadow, like Seeta's, continued to fall on the decades to come. Even the more creative directors fell under its influence—Raj Kapoor in *Aah* about a tuberculous patient deliberately staying away from his true love and Guru Dutt in *Pyaasa* telling the tale of a poet's yearning for fame and love, with his poetry going unpublished, his beloved married to a rich man and a prostitute giving him solace. This pattern also provided the genesis for the eternal triangles (some expanded to quadrilaterals) found in a countless number of films. Mehboob's *Andaz* (1949) extended it to the Westernised girl ruining her marriage due to the 'mistake' of having a male friend.

The conflict in love comes in the form of parental opposition, class or other differences, the villain's machinations, tribal feuds or an illness, self-inflicted or natural. It took various patterns, all of them lucrative: *Mela, Ratan, Nagin, Aar Paar, Deedar, Anmol Ghadi*, etc. It assumed a different style in Raj Kapoor's *Barsaat*, which people called the caveman style of loving, but came back to the same type in his *Bobby*, a story of teenage love and elopement with parents rattling the sabres. *Love Story* was re-discovered for *Ankhiyon Ke Jharonkhon Se* with the college girl dying of blood cancer, an addition being that she is a Christian and the boy a Hindu. Stoicism in the face of a fatal disease was popularised in Hrishikesh Mukherji's *Anand*, played by Rajesh Khanna who became a much-loved star for a time. Its female version with versatile Jaya Bhaduri in the role was *Mili* by the same director, who is rated among the few who make a better kind of Hindi film.

Re-birth and amnesia are other contrivances by which romance rises and fades and perhaps rises again. The Indian tradition of reincarnation is twisted to keep the stars lovers throughout their various births and sometimes turn them into ghosts, singing haunting songs, in haunted mansions. Even a high-calibre director Bimal Roy could not resist making *Madhumati* on this idea with big stars in the lead.

On the last rung are the stories of love for animals, who become central characters and sometimes even threaten the human love affair. South's producer Sandow Devar specialised in them, making regular heroes or heroines out of elephants, dogs, cows and also a goat. The testing point

Jaya Bhaduri as the ebullient girl dying of an incurable disease in *Mili*.

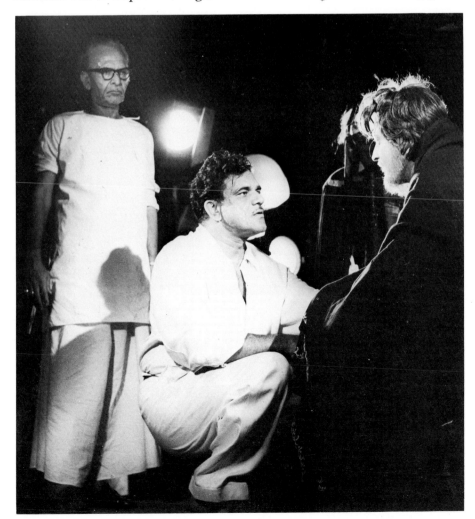

The director K. Asif talks to Guru Dutt during the making of *Love and God*, which he died without completing.

39

Snake worship at its most ridiculous in *Shub Din*, 1973.

Internationally-known dancer Uday Shankar (the brother of Ravi Shankar) in his only dance-based film, *Kalpana*, 1948.

was *Shub Din* where cobras have a rapport with the heroine. And when one reptile kisses the girl's lips in a close-up, it must have sent shudders down the system of the most devout of snake worshippers.

MUSIC and DANCE

Romance is, of course, linked to songs. That way, critics always cry themselves hoarse that every type of Indian film is a musical since each must have the trade-demanded quota of songs. Only a few have evaded it by minimising the songs or putting them into the background. The totally songless films are isolated landmarks which stand out from the thousands produced. J. B. H. Wadia's *Navjawan*, K. A. Abbas' *Munna*, B. R. Chopra's *Kanoon* and *Ittefaq*, a wordless Bengali film *Ingeet* and a Tamil film *Antha Naal* are among those to claim this negative honour. Later Satyajit Ray's and other regional films as also some avant-garde ones succeeded in doing away with songs, but now once again they are conceded to, except by the most uncompromising directors like Ray or Mrinal Sen.

The film song (often a thing of wonder for non-Indians) is like a dream, irrelevant to the film, when everything else stands suspended except the wish or the emotion being expressed. Many songs on discs extend beyond the films and leave a deep impact on self-identification. Songs arrived in Indian Cinema right from the first talkie *Alam Ara* as a tradition lifted straight from the stage. The biggest hits among early talkies had a large number of songs, from 20 to 40, and in *Indra Sabha* it reached the staggering figure of 71. Even the best among the popular films made in later decades relied on songs as an important aid. A separate disc industry, unlinked with films, did not spring up so the tradition crystallised and now nobody questions when a song crops up in the most unlikely situation.

Songs reached their height in the romantic films of the 1940s and 1950s, though the essentials of a real musical were rarely seen except in a few films where the characters were singers on the radio or the stage or a quite recent film *Heer Ranjah* where the whole dialogue is in a lyrical-musical form. But there came a time when composers like Naushad and C. Ramchandra were at their peak and so entire films became music-orientated, with the scripts built to lead up to the songs. Gradually, the songs have declined, to some extent in number and a large extent in quality. At present, an average of four to five occur in every kind of film, though their importance in the film varies. Still the few top composers charge high fees, like the few playback singers. And perhaps this is the only cinema in the world where music directors get equal billing with the directors.

Wholly dance-based films have been a rarity. The concoction of a little of everything seldom allows such specialised developments. In 1948, the internationally famed Uday Shankar made his first and last film, *Kalpana*, woven entirely in dance numbers. V. Shantaram's *Jhanak Jhanak Paayal Baaje*, the first shot in Technicolor by Indian technicians, can also claim credit in this genre. But, by and large, dance as an art form or a province-based form of expression has occurred in separately conceived items just like music. They are part of the whole but never the whole.

A folksong and folk-dance from *Jhoola,* with Mumtaz Ali and Azurie in Bombay Talkies' 1941 film about lovers facing parental and class opposition.

Themes of Conflict and Collaboration

FAMILY DRAMA

The wide range of socials covers various problems in and out of the family. The need for keeping the family together as a unit has led to various plots involving all the domestic characters. Those who have broken away from the family are the outcasts, often becoming the law-breaker in the crime film. As a threat to the unity of the family, taken as the smallest unit and symbolising the larger one of the country, are the multiple conflicts between communities, provinces, classes, castes and between cultures in general.

The family drama has been as much a staple diet as the myth. The basic conflict is between the joint family as laid down by the country's tradition and the independent household spurred by influences of the West. Film-makers have portrayed the problems in their different aspects, but in conclusion they have preferred to sit on the fence although usually implying support for the extended family. This appeases tradition and ensures the approval of the predominantly conservative audience. The status quo must be maintained, even though the writers and directors themselves may not believe in it or practise it themselves.

The joint family generates various difficulties, especially for the raw young daughter-in-law, who gets the worst of the bargain. Whatever the genre or period of the film, she suffers untold miseries and sometimes gets harassed and enslaved like an animal. But in the end when she gets her long-deserved due, she herself pleads for the pardon of her tormentors and for bringing them back into the family fold. However much the family may break up or be separated by distance or calamity, the re-union is a must. Economic factors are involved too, since the large family means conservation of property and land. In a certain sect in the South, the tradition is for the eldest son's wife to be treated as theirs by the younger brothers. Perhaps Draupadi in Mahabharata having five husbands is not just a myth.

One of the earliest films to tackle the eternal clash between the new bride and mother-in-law was *Charnon Ki Daasi* (Slave at the feet) written by P. K. Atre, a noted Marathi author, and directed by G. Jagirdar in Hindi and Marathi. It gave such a horrific picture of the whole thing that the unconventional protest was fairly clear. A little later, Atre's own production *Raja Rani* made a comedy out of a couple fed up with life in a joint family. They set up their own home, but the problems are even bigger so they return to the big house. In the 1970s an excellent tragicomedy was made in Marathi, *Mumbaicha Jawai* (Son-in-law in Bombay), remade in Hindi as *Piya Ka Ghar* (Husband's home), where a new couple living in a single-room tenement with a lower middle class family find it impossible to make love and realise that even the family head has to go out for that to a lodging house. Finally, they decide to stay with the family. Basu Chatterji, who made his 'new wave' debut with *Sara Akash*, also dealt with problems of adjustments of a young bride with her hostile husband and big family.

Domestic characters have provided scope for various types of dramas in films. Fights between brothers, instigated by their wives, lead to division of property and the erection of partitions in the house until the final tearful come-together. Children are separated from parents for some reason and grow up in the big city, often as people of different communities and professions; brothers happen to stand on opposite sides of the law until the identities are sorted out and all come together (with the communities now forgotten). This theme, used recently in more than 50 films in a short span, again yielded a big hit in Manmohan Desai's *Amar Akbar Anthony*, having top stars and seasoned with all the stuff usually described as 'masala' (cliche spices). Another fertile field is the clash of different relationships in a family, a delicate one being between the younger brother and sister-in-law whose affection is suspected. Kitchen quarrels provide yet another rich source.

Love for the sister expressed through the Indian custom of 'raakhee' (a ceremonial thread tied by a sister on the brother's hand assuring her protection) has also led to many tear-jerking melodramas such as *Meri Bahen* and *Chhoti Bahen*. An example of how genres can overlap is in a historical, *Humayun*, where the 'raakhee' idea was used for a Hindu princess to seek the help of the Mughal king. In *Tapasya* it is the elder sister who gives every sacrifice for the sake of her orphaned brother and sisters. Only in a rare case, Mehboob's *Bahen* (Sister), was the excessive obsession of a tall, hefty brother for his maidenly sister tackled, but on a subdued note.

A symbolical image of the tall, hefty brother and his beloved kid sister for whom he has a morbid obsession in Mehboob's *Bahen*, 1941.

The humble nature of the Indian bride was taken to melodramatic extremes in films such as *Gumasta*, 1951.

Films about 'Maa', Bahen' and 'Ghar' (mother, sister, and home) have always been popular. The fashionable wife from the city creates problems for the boy's mother and sister who are neglected. The wife is made out to be a vamp and the contrast provided by another couple with a very understanding wife. The pattern proved a big hit in S. M. Yusuf's *Grahasthi* (1948). In the 1970s the idea of two such couples has been tried again in *Swarg Narak* by producer Nagi Reddi, of Vijaya Vauhini Studios of Madras, the biggest in Asia. The idea of a Plain Jane losing her husband to the other woman and then getting her back proved a gold mine when Chandulal Shah discovered it in the silent era as *Gunsundari* with a revealing alternative title, *Why Husbands Go Astray*, (the answer being that wives are not what they should be). It was made as a talkie and again re-made, each time with success. Shantaram made a superb social fantasy of it — the poet husband creates a glamorous split personality of his own unattractive wife and 'lives' with her in *Navrang*.

But the real biting problem about extra marital relations has not been touched in its gravity. B. R. Chopra's *Gumrah* (One lost on the way) showed a woman married to an elderly man, attracted again by her previous lover. However, it was then quickly changed into a suspense plot about blackmail. At the film's end, when the man comes asking for the girl by her first name, she replies that there is only Mrs. so and so living there and closes the door. In 1977, Chopra tried again in *Pati Patni Aur Woh* (Husband, wife and she) by making it into a mild comedy with no serious damage done. Marital incompatibility is becoming somewhat of an obsession for some avant-garde film makers; Basu Bhattacharya made some intellectual films on it with *Anubhav, Aavishkar* and *Grihapravesh* (Experience, discovery and home-entry) with the couples realising their folly. In other films, divorce has been discussed and also gone through, but the moralist in the Indian Cinema has always worked out a re-union. *Yeh Raaste Hain Pyar Ke* (Such are the paths of love) took up a real-life case of a navy man shooting down a businessman who had illicit relations with his wife, but diluted it with songs and the suggestion of the wife making a one-night blunder, being intoxicated and seduced. Satyajit Ray took a totally different track in *Kapurush* (The coward). The former lover is a coward and the married couple prove him to be so all over again.

CRIME DRAMA

The crime film has never really been a part of the Indian reality, being lifted straight from the Hollywood films which were imported in large numbers. They were, of course, garnished with the typical icings of Indian films, including singing girls and dancing dolls as the second heroines, while keeping the morality intact. The hero could flirt, sing and dance with them but no more. It has to be a one-woman affair or else he becomes a villain in the audience's eyes.

Crime had actually taken quite an early and original start as a silent film *Kala Naag* (Black cobra) in 1924. Directed by Homi Master who also played the title role, it was based on the career of an actual criminal who had terrorised Bombay and it promised to show robberies, murders and rapes. The film was received so well that Master came up with a sequel *Return of Kala Naag*. In the talkies it was *Kismet*, about a lovable thief, who does a lot of good and turns out to be the boy of a good family. The film became a terrific hit, songs and all, scoring a record nonstop run of nearly four years in Calcutta.

At other times, non-Indian literature provided meat for Indian crime drama; *Jail Yatra* (Jail term) was based on *Les Miserables*, *Duniya Kya Hai* (What's this world) on *Resurrection* and *Phir Subaha Hogi* (It will be dawn again) on *Crime and Punishment*. Star Dev Anand under his banner Navketan and Guru Dutt who was producer, director and actor specialised in a likable kind of urban crime thriller, which also improved over the love theme. Here, the hero did not grow sad and moody at setbacks in love but sang merry songs, took life as it came and got the beloved as a matter of course. These films — *Baazi* (Gamble), *Aar Paar* (Across the heart), *C.I.D.* and others set a new trend in making films more cinematic and alluring.

In all this, the reform of criminals was rarely considered, an exception being V. Shantaram's *Do Ankhen Barah Haath* (Two eyes, twelve hands) which had its jailor hero experimenting in an open air jail, for six hardened convicts whom he transforms. The film won awards abroad despite the inevitable songs and other extraneous elements. Another offshoot of crime drama was the dacoit drama, for example *Ganga Jamna*, *Jis Desh Mein Ganga Behti Hai* (The country in which Ganges flows) and *Mujhe Jeene Do* (Cry For Life). In recent years, this has reaped a large harvest of crude dacoit films with the hero as the much wronged wrongdoer. Another outcome is the 'curry Western', best represented by the unbelievably successful *Sholay* (Flames), which had a retired police officer hiring gunmen with a jail record to bust a dacoit gang terrorising a lonely village. Crime dramas, too, have taken various violent forms, showing kidnappings, ransom demands, killings and all, which have inspired actual cases, the criminals acknowledging the source when questioned after arrest. While crime is shown, its necessary concommitants of crime detection and police work are seldom gone into in any detail.

OTHER CONFLICTS

A favourite pastime of film makers is to pit one belief or group against another, though usually on a superficial level, especially if it treads on sensitive spots and always ending in an ultimate message of harmony. One subject is the intercommunal conflict, still a thorny problem in India, cropping up at any provocation. The need for Hindus and Muslims (films seldom feature other communities) to live in peace after the country's partition has always been acute and if films have helped, then we must give them their due. The message, even if corny, has always been packed in, through the dialogue, songs, sub-plots etc. even if the film's main storyline has little to do with it.

A fully-fledged, successful attempt was made by V. Shantaram in *Padosi* (Neighbour), also filmed in Marathi in 1941. It was an allegory with an Hindu and a Muslim family in a village living side by side in great

Mujhe Jeene Do is one of many dacoit dramas which have been made recently. It starred Sunil Dutt and Waheeda Rehman.

mutual attachment (symbolised by their chess-board) until disruptive forces from outside create a rift leading to a tragic death of the two old men. The producer made the theme more real by using a Hindu actor to do the Muslim character and a Muslim to play the Hindu role. Prabhat's *Hum Ek Hain* (We are one), directed by Santoshi, had a mother-image (India) nurturing boys of three communities. Later, B.R. Chopra in *Dharamputra* (A son by faith) took the exceptional case of an illegitimate child growing up to be a fanatical Hindu and discovering at the height of his hate campaign that he is a Muslim by birth. The audience resented the film. In other cases, intercommunal love has been portrayed, but marriage always evaded. This is more feasible with other minority communities like Anglo-Indians, as done quite realistically in Nagi Reddi's *Julie*, re-made from a Malayalam film. The inter-religious clash points were also brought out.

The fake kind of communal integration has always existed in box-office films, with the Hindu singing a bhajan, the Muslim a quawali and the Christian a song like *My name is Anthony Gonsalvez*. Interaction between the large number of religious and language speaking groups has been on a breezy, comic level. Marwaris, Sindhis, Parsis or South Indians are made to wear their old hereditary dress and speak in the particular lingo though times have changed and actual integration is much further advanced, at least in appearances. The cinema's bid is to cater to all tastes, which started with antics like 'namaste' to the Hindu, 'salaam' to the Muslim, 'sat siri akal' to the Sikh and well, to the Christian, 'good morning' for want of anything better. There is also the multilingual song, with each verse written in a different language. Recently, Basu Chatterji made *Khatta Meetha* (Sour-sweet) centering on the small Parsi community without probing into it. The idea was to adapt a Turkish film about the late marriage of a widow and a widower with children. The progressive and Westernised Parsis could find acceptance doing such a thing which would be unthinkable for other bigger communities.

Inter-provincial mixing is another theme which has been analysed in various plots. In Mohan Sehgal's *New Delhi* it was through a North-South love affair and marriage, after overcoming parental opposition. In V. Shantaram's *Teen Batti Char Rasta* (Three lamps, at the cross roads) it was a stylistic pattern of a big family having six daughters-in-law from different regions. In K.A. Abbas' *Saat Hindustani* (Seven Indians) men from different provinces join hands to fight for the liberation of Goa from the Portuguese and become full Indians for a time.

Padosi (Neighbour) was a strong plea for Hindu-Muslim unity. Mazharkhan (left) played the Hindu neighbour and Jagirdar (right) the Muslim; their friendship was symbolised by the chess board.

The inter-caste issue, especially in relation to the lower, depressed, untouchable ones has found reasonably good expression from the early days. *Chandidas* directed by Nitin Bose was the tale of the poet-priest, who forsook the order for the love of a washerwoman. Untouchability has been castigated in many films including Shantaram's *Dharmatma*, Chandulal Shah's *Achhoot*, Bombay Talkies' *Achhoot Kanya* (Untouchable girl), Bimal Roy's *Sujata*, Vasant Joglekar's *Prarthna* (Plea) and Abbas' *Char Dil Char Raahen* (Four hearts and their paths). A new anti-Brahminist wave has spread in South's films following the Kannada *Samskara*. Recent Hindi movies on the subject are Rajinder Singh Bedi's *Aankhin Dekhi* (Eye-witnessed) and Kidar Sharma's *Pahela Kadam* (The first step). The main thrust in most Hindi films is a Brahmin-Harijan romance, but other problems like temple entry, filling water from the common well and conversion to Christianity are also discussed.

The rural-urban contrast has provided another theme for numerous films, the general attitude being that everything to do with the village is good and everything to do with the city is bad. The yokel coming to town has been a favourite source of comedy, though he proves smarter than the town people by winning the heart of the up-to-date heroine. Recently some serious themes on migration have been taken up; K. Balachander's Tamil *Pattina Pravesam* (Entry in the city) and Muzaffar Ali's *Gaman* (Transition) being two films which deal with this topic.

The East versus West conflict has provided more grist to the mill. It arose from the patriotic fervour of fighting the alien rule and continues from the fear of any foreign cultural onslaught. Films usually play the double game of highlighting all the glamour and glitter of the Occidental ways of life before condemning them and stressing the need to remain Indian. Depiction of non-Indians and Westernised Indians has mostly been a lopsided one. Villains and vamps were those dressed in foreignish costumes and the concept of a Westernised woman is still a smoking, drinking, scantily-clad one. If the heroine wears a mini-skirt or dances to Western tunes, nothing much is lost so long as she remains a one-man woman, as the hero is expected to be a one-woman man. Only the baddies can ask for more. In recent times, leading film maker cum star Manoj Kumar has made it a credo to support the Indian stand against the foreign with a missionary zeal in his films *Upkar* (Obligation), *Purab Aur Paschim* (East and West), *Roti Kapda Aur Makaan* (Food, clothing, shelter) and *Kranti* (Revolution) set in the days of the Indian Mutiny.

COLLABORATION

On another level, producers and actors have always made attempts to go semi-West, either by shooting abroad, participating in productions of other countries or attempting joint or co-productions, though success has been only intermittent.

In 1924, Madan Theatres of Calcutta which had Italians and French on its staff, made *Savitri* jointly with U.C. Italiana of Rome and featured

Light of Asia, 1926, was a co-production with the Emelka Film Company of Munich and starred Himansu Rai as Prince Siddhartha and the Anglo-Indian actress Sita Devi as his queen.

Rina de Liguoro and Angelo Ferrari as the mythical Hindu characters, Savitri and Satyawan. It was produced in Italy under the supervision of Arturo Ambrosio (director of *Theodara* and *Last Days of Pompeii*), with indoor filming at Rome's Cine Studios and outdoor filming at the Cascade of Trivoli, palace of Count Chiggi and the Frascati, which considering the Indian divine tale must have become a terrible combination indeed. Other roles were played by Bruto Castellani, Mastripiztri and Signorita Terribilli. Earlier, Madan's *Laila Majnu* had British artists Jeanette Sherwin and H.B. Waring appearing as the legendary lovers.

Himansu Rai achieved a more reasonable balance when he made *Light of Asia* with the Emelka Film Company of Munich. The shooting was done wholly in India at some excellent authentic locales, with Rai playing prince Siddhartha (who became Buddha) and an Anglo-Indian actress Sita Devi as his queen. The post-shooting work was done in Germany, the company having provided finance, equipment and craftsmen like director Franz Osten, who later joined Rai when he formed Bombay Talkies. Response to the hybrid production was cool in India, but it had major openings in European cities and a Royal Command performance at Windsor Castle, where the Queen complimented Rai and writer Niranjan Pal. Perhaps coincidentally, in London the film achieved a good run. The *Daily Express* called it one of the best films of the year. Then Rai made *Shiraz* for U.F.A. of Germany and British Instructional Films of England, a story of how the Taj Mahal was built, followed by *A Throw of Dice* made with U.F.A. and Bruce Wolf of U.K. about two princes in love with the same woman.

When talking pictures came, Rai made *Karma* (Fate) jointly with I.B.B. of England, directed by J. L. Freer Hunt and scripted by Rupert Downing with music by Ernest Broadhurst. It was in English and Hindi with one English song. The outdoor filming was done in India, but the indoor work was shot at Stoll Studios in London. This time, acting opposite Rai in his last screen appearance was his charming wife, Devika Rani, who was related to Rabindranath Tagore. They played royal heirs who wanted their rival kingdoms modernised, the lean story of maharajas being propped up by elephants, tigers, snakes and screen kisses. Still, the unusual nature of the production and the zeal of the Indian enterprise earned acclaim for it in other countries. The premiere was held at London's Marble Arch Pavilion and the press went out of its way to welcome it. Reviews in the *Sunday Chronicle*, *Sunday Times* and *Sunday Pictorial* were the kind of raves which Indian producers would die for. Devika Rani was given the privilege of broadcasting three B.B.C. sessions. In India, it fared badly though Sarojini Naidu and others spoke

Non-Indian stars have been much sought after for Indian films. Soviet ballerina Rabienkina appeared in Raj Kapoor's *Mera Naam Joker* with a complete Soviet circus troupe!

The kiss was seen in early Indian Cinema as in *Karma*, an Indo-British co-production directed by and starring Himansu Rai with Devika Rani.

in favour of it at the opening. After that, Rai set up a typically Indian concern named Bombay Talkies to make typically Indian films and at last succeeded in a big way. East had won and West had lost.

There are also some other collaboration ventures worth a mention. *Shikari* (Hunter) shot in India was produced by Captain F. W. Pitt, directed by Naval Gandhi and scripted by C. L. Reed and Adrian Brunel. Sita Devi and Jairaj led the cast. *Emerald of the East* was produced by British International Studios on Indian locations and adapted from a story by an Indian lady novelist. Later years have seen Dev Anand's *Guide* having an English version co-produced with Pearl Buck and Tad Danielewski. K. A. Abbas made a big co-production *Pardesi* (Foreigner) in colour with Mosfilm Studios, shot both in India and Soviet Russia. Once again, audience response in India was lukewarm. It was a travelogue about a Russian traveller's visit to ancient India. In each department, an Indian and a Russian joined hands to illustrate the spirit of integration. Raj Kapoor's *Mera Naam Joker* (I am a clown) included a Soviet ballerina and an entire circus troupe for one of the three episodes.

English versions, exchange of artists and shooting in other countries have been other ways of trying to make an international dent and get wider markets, other than the traditional foreign ones of Indians settled abroad. In 1941, J. B. H. Wadia made *Court Dancer* or *Raj Nartaki* in Hindi, Bengali and also English, the last being a special version meant for a world market which it could not reach due to the wartime handicaps. Other films in English spurred by the innovation of colour were *Jhansi Ki Rani*, *Pamposh* directed by Ezra Mir for producer Ambalal Patel, which was made in German too and G. P. Sippy's *Shahenshah* (Queen of Araby). Some down-to-earth black and white films done in English were Abbas' *Rahi* (Traveller) and Datta Dharmadhikari's *Mahatma* (The great soul). Finally, Ismail Merchant and James Ivory made *Householder, Shakespearewallah, Bombay Talkie* and *Guru*, with the active cooperation of star

above
A typical fantasy song and dance in *Jal Bin Machhli, Nritya Bin Bijli*.

opposite
Hema Malini, a top-ranking star and expert Bharat Natyam dancer, in a dance scene from *Mrig Trishna*.

right
Court Dancer, a film in English by J. B. H. Wadia and starring Prithviraj Kapoor and Sadhna Bose.

Shashi Kapoor who had already acted in international productions as had I. S. Johar and Kabir Bedi. In 1978-79 Rex Harrison visited India for Krishna Shah's Indo-American film *Shalimar* and Indian stars worked in the U.S.S.R. for F. C. Mehra's co-production *Alibaba*. The idea of having foreign locations for typically Indian films was started by Raj Kapoor's *Sangam* (Confluence), a routine love yarn. It soon became a formula and producers got busy shooting songs, dances, fights and chases all over the world, much to the amazement of the 'world'.

Social Concern

Indian Cinema's attempts to tackle some of the burning social, socio-economic and political problems are to be commended, if only because the audience usually shies away from them and makes it plain that what it wants is escapism and whatever goes under the vague label of entertainment, at least in the all-India cinema.

That is why national films have always wrapped any problems they dealt with in the sugar coating of songs, dances, dramatic dialogue, comic sequences and so on for easier and wider consumption. This has not been so in the regional art films and a few other exceptions. It was also not so true in the older films, when the stakes were smaller and the audience more serious and responsive. So the big banners of the 1930s and 1940s (New Theatres, Prabhat, Bombay Talkies, Minerva, National Studios, Ranjit, Sagar, Kardar, Filmistan, Wadia Brothers and Rajkamal) could try out a variety of themes, even if framed in a popularly enjoyable set-up.

Stories about the oldest 'professionals' provide a typical study. In the silent films such women were roundly condemned as home-wreckers, gold-diggers and disease-spreaders. This notion was carried forward by hits of which *Gunsundari* was typical. Later it was rejected in favour of a more humane approach to the prostitute, as a woman with her own emotions and hopes, more sinned against than sinning, with the blame for her plight shifted to 'samaj' (Society) meaning the males. This was so in *Devdas* and more sharply marked in V. Shantaram's *Aadmi* (Man). But the crucial problem of her rehabilitation in a domestic household was always stalled, in a this-far-and-no-further concession to public acceptance. The prostitute coming inside the house was just a bit too much. She could be glorified better by death or permanent exile.

Even in B. R. Ishara's *Chetana* (Awakening) made with all the 'new wave' zeal and a lot of cheeky display of flesh and slang talk, the end has

Aadmi, 1941, was one of the first films to treat the plight of the prostitute in humane terms.

right
Chetana was a 'new wave' film shot in 1970.

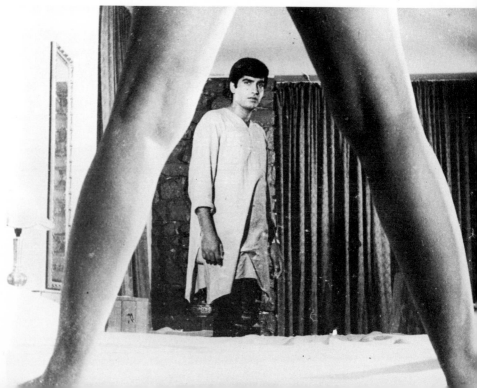

52

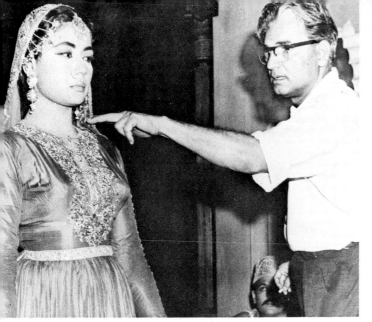

to be tragic. Yet films like B. R. Chopra's *Sadhana* (Longing) and the Malayalam film *Her Nights* have shown a happy marriage, while *Pyaasa* (Thirst) had the prostitute renouncing society with the hero. Hitting at the roots of the system itself was *Prabhat* (Dawn), but it was too harsh and rough to get acceptance. A safe but laughable ruse is to keep the girl a mere singer-dancer (and hence virgin) even if she tumbles through a dozen brothels. So her marriage path is easy and the audience goes home with a clean conscience.

Somewhat less tarnished socially are the characters of stage dancers, singers, those in the traditional folk troupes known as 'tamasha' or 'nautanki', circus artists, gypsies, singers of quawalis (a form of Urdu musical poetry) and even cinema's own directors and actors. Snobbish opposition to their mixing in good society is brought from the moralists and older generation, but is generally overcome. Guru Dutt made quite a poignant film on the fickle and despised life of a film maker in *Kaagaz Ke Phool* (Paper flowers). *Sone Ki Chidiya* (Golden goose) on the life of a young female star, *Guddi* (Lass) on a teenage girl's crush on matinee idol Dharmendra who appears as himself and *Bhumika* (The role) inspired from the life of a free-living actress Hansa Wadkar who wrote her autobiography before death are all good films. Satyajit Ray had the last word with *Nayak* (The hero) starring Bengal's top hero, Uttam Kumar. A peculiarity is that the audience resents films about films and the breaking of the screen illusion. Sucking the lollipop is more important than seeing how it is made.

The special problems of women and children have also motivated various films, though these themes are normally only a part of the entertaining whole. A woman's talent being neglected by domestic drudgery or a careless husband or father and her being drawn to a former sympathiser have yielded good films among which are Hrishikesh Mukherji's *Anuradha, Anupama* (both proper names) and *Abhimaan* (Pride) where there is a clash of egos between a gifted husband and wife, and, of course, Ray's masterpiece *Charulata*. The problems of a busy doctor-wife and her lawyer-husband, adapted from K. M. Munshi's novel, were tackled way back in 1935 in *Dr. Madhurika*, with a traditionally satisfying end. Women's literacy, progress and independence have been advocated, though only up to a limit. Women's lib has not really arrived, except through vamps. The domestic task, after all, is equally important. But a remarkable film *Amar Jyoti* (Immortal flame) in a costume-period garb was tried by Shantaram in 1936. A fiery woman pirate takes it out on men by enslaving them, punishing them and firing other women with the same spirit. The film succeeded but the trend ended there.

opposite
Young love is always popular at the box-office. *Bobby* was directed by Raj Kapoor and starred his son Rishi Kapoor and Dimple in her first and last film.

above
The Christian girl Ranjeeta and the Hindu boy Sachin are a pair of star-crossed lovers in *Ankhiyon Ke Jharonkhon Se.*

left
Tarana, 1979, starred Ranjeeta and Mithun Chakravarty in a story about the love between a gypsy girl and an aristocratic boy.

Sindoor, a film about widow re-marriage.

right
The Unexpected was a remarkable protest against arranged marriages. Shanta Apte played a young girl wedded to an old man who refuses to accept him.

below
A child bride learns about marriage. A scene from the sensitive Bengali film *Balika Badhu*, 1966.

Kept hidden under a veil are touchy issues like 'sati', the obsolete custom of widows throwing themselves on the husband's pyre, which are given a veiled suggestion in songs and dialogue or in historicals as a self-sacrifice against enemy take-over. But child marriage and widow re-marriage have been dealt with, combining both protest and convention. Thus a marriage or arrangement made in childhood may be condemned, but with some twists and turns of romance it turns out to be the right choice. A series of very successful films have been made by Nasir Hussein from *Jab Pyar Kisi Se Hota Hai* (When you love someone) to the 1978 hit *Hum Kisise Kam Nahin* (I am no less than anyone) around the same formula of boy and girl engaged in childhood, later thwarted by parents and turning out to be the ideal pair. The big audience response shows that they inwardly like child marriages, as they also do love stories beginning right from the kids billing, cooing and singing. Surprisingly, the films are a big hit with the young audience also. Perhaps, in a restrictive society, they too find it tough to do partner hunting and prefer the old arranged bond.

In Kardar's *Sharda* (1942), the issue of child marriage leading to an ill-matched pair and much misery was treated in a light vein. Earlier silent films had projected the grave problem, in the wake of which laws were passed to prohibit it. Young widows getting re-married was strongly advocated in *Sindoor* which was directed by Kishore Sahu for Filmistan. There had been films before on child widows, too. And in 1977, the top national award winner *Ghatashraddha* in Kannada brought out the antique rural custom of giving a living death to widows suspected to be immoral. A related issue is the bargain marriage of very young girls to very old men. After some early protest films, this was given its most powerful shake-up in Shantaram's *Duniya Na Mane* (1937) called *The Unexpected* in English. Taking the basic plot of a Marathi novel, the film strengthened it further by removing the love element and making it the straight fight of the brave determined girl who refuses to accept the old man as her husband, in any sense. After every possible effort to tame her, he submits by accepting her as his daughter, entreating her to re-marry and committing suicide. It still remains one of the most remarkable films in the history of national Hindi Cinema and so too Shanta Apte's performance in the role.

On the other hand the idea of girls prematurely going through a marriage and then realising its sexual implications has received a light-

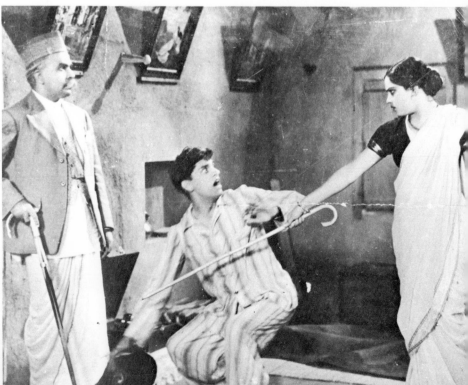

hearted treatment. Taking the cue from the Tagore story, Ray turned it
into the delightful piece *Samaapti* (part of *Two Daughters*) re-made in
Hindi as *Uphaar* (Gift). Tarun Majumdar made the Bengali *Balika Badhu*
(also re-made in Hindi) though it does seem an odd idea for the 'child
bride' to go to the erotic monuments of Khajuraho or Konarak to find
what marriage is all about. The battle of the sexes has also taken other
comic forms, the extreme being *Ulti Ganga* (Reverse flow) made in 1942,
where women take over all the functions of men who look after the
house.

Fantasies apart, other customary handicaps of women have not been
grappled with and on the contrary have been exploited romantically. For
example, the 'ghunghat' (for Hindu) and 'pardah' (for Muslim) enjoining
on women to keep their faces covered has been fought against by
women's welfare and other organisations, but the cinema has not dared
to raise a protest except in plots such as one man's new bride being taken
away by another by mistake or the pardah making a Muslim lover marry
off his beloved to his best friend and then becoming aghast, leading to
tragedy. One hero even wooed the wrong girl because he identified her
more from the dupatta (scarf) than the face, till the heroine donned the
right scarf.

top
The 'ghunghat' for the orthodox
women is seldom protested against.
Here Smita Patil dons it as a village
woman in Shyam Benegal's *Manthan*.

above
Meena Kumari in 'pardah' and so
hidden from Sunil Dutt in *Ghazal*.

Dowry is another acute problem, usually employed for a dramatic
sequence of the boy's father taking back the 'baraat' (marriage party)
from the ceremonial shamiana' A fully-fledged tirade was made by V.
Shantaram in *Dahej* (Dowry) made in 1950. Despite its patches of shrill
melodrama, the film painted such a scary and tragic picture of the evil
that it must have led to some change of heart somewhere if written
reaction is to be believed. Films have also kept away from the more
gruesome aspects, reported often in the papers, such as setting fire to the

57

above
The current top male star Amitabh Bachchan (front) and the famous actor Pran in a formula scene of violence from the Hindi crime film *Don* about a villager taking a dead smuggler's place.

right
The eternal triangle in B. R. Chopra's comedy *Pati Patni Aur Woh*.

below right
Ittefaq was also directed by Chopra and was a songless crime drama with Rajesh Khanna and Nanda.

opposite
Raakhee (centre) as the oldest sister who sacrifices her own happiness to help her sisters marry. The film was *Tapasya*.

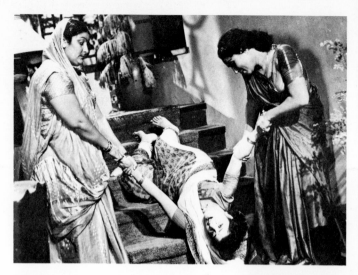

above
V. Shantaram made a scorching attack on the evil of dowries in *Dahej*, 1950.

above right
Shree 420, 1955, was a Chaplinesque satire by Raj Kapoor.

right
The wife cowed into submission by the threat of a second wife—a scene from *Doosri Shaadi*, 1947.

below
A successful children's film, *Boot Polish* had David Abraham as the bootlegger and Baby Naaz and Rattan Kumar as the derelict children.

daughters-in-law or suicide by the girls in this fashion. About bigamy, though laws are passed, the men in films often suppress and browbeat women with the eternal threat of the second wife or mistress, usually for failure to beget a child. Often the woman herself offers the great sacrifice of accepting the second woman. Only in a 1978 film, Raj Khosla's *Main Tulsi Tere Aangan Ki* (I am the plant in your courtyard) has the conflict been given a humane form, where the wife becomes eternally obliged to the mistress and her child, because of the ultimate sacrifice of suicide which the mistress gives.

Illegitimate children provide another source of sentimental melodrama in which children grow up in different homes and circumstances, only discovering their parents at the end. But there is a skirting of the real problem of children forsaken or left in destitute homes and the kind of life they grow into without ever being claimed by their parents. Even then, there have been attempts to portray the suffering, both of parents and children and using the opportunity to put the child above the barriers of community or caste, making him a real Indian. A good example was B. R. Chopra's *Dhool Ka Phool* (Blossom in the dust) directed by Yash Chopra in 1959 which had many unusual elements including an anti-hero, who ditches his pregnant girl and marries another. Like most Hindi films, the story goes through a three-hour-long drama of twists and turns, songs and sundry other standard situations without which, perhaps, the movie would not have been such a big success.

Other themes about children have covered many aspects, a general complaint being that the child is seldom natural, but an over-wise, precocious and often terrible brat, who is made to act like a performing animal. It seems that audiences adore the super-child and derive satisfaction from the screen-image, perhaps some vicarious pleasure, too, from the child's 'innocent vulgarity'. Two sisters, Daisy and Honey Irani, doing impossible acts and setting right the erring elders, became very popular in the 1950s and established an even more rigid formula. Chaplin's *The Kid* also had its counterparts with *Mastana* (Happy-go-lucky) in 1954 and *Kunwara Baap* (Unwed father) in 1974. In the latter, the issue of polio was quite well integrated into the typical light-comedy of comedian Mehmood.

A call by the then Prime Minister Pandit Nehru in the 1950s to make films for children brought forth a spate of them. The only catch was that film makers could not distinguish between films for children and films about children. Consequently, many of them dealt with adult problems while having children as central characters who brought about changes in the grown-ups and their various vices, desires or fears. No wonder that the trend did not permit the growth of a healthy children's film movement, but films such as *Munna* (Child), *Boot Polish, Ab Dilli Door Nahin* (Delhi is not far off now) at least did focus on the plight of children left at the mercy of the world, an eye-opener for the more privileged classes and the government itself. Bimal Roy made quite a poignant Indian version of *Simon's Papa* in *Baap Beti* (Father and daughter) featuring Baby Tabassum and Ranjan. Later, *Jagriti* (Awakening) directed by Satyen Bose with shades of *Mr. Chips*, made a fairly serious study of the educational system and classroom problems, although later films in the same vein were poor. In the 1970s Gulzar's *Kitaab* (Book) was once again a child film for adults.

Physical and mental handicaps have been dealt with as individual rather than social problems. Still *Parichay* (Acquaintance), made in 1954, was a worthwhile film about a deaf and dumb bride palmed off to a man who gradually realises her virtues. Much later, Gulzar's *Koshish* (Attempt) seemed to put the plight of a deaf and dumb couple on a wider social plane, except that it lifted its inspiration from the Japanese

Baby Naaz

overleaf top left
A crime-dacoit drama, *Kachche Dhaage* with Kabir Bedi (right), Vinod Khanna and Moushumi Chatterjee.

overleaf bottom left
Parsis depicted in colourful gaiety in *Khatta Meetha.*

overleaf right
Amitabh Bachchan in *Amar Akbar Anthony.*

61

A scene from *Parbat Pe Apna Dera.*

Happiness of Us Alone, which can be taken as one of the major disadvantages of holding international film festivals in India. Blindness has become another handy device for creating sympathy or romanticising, with leading stars adopting it, just like wearing glasses to look differently attractive or intellectual.

Mental imbalance has usually been treated romantically or comically, a serious exception being *Swayam Siddha*, (Self-accomplished) 1949, which showed a dominant woman, married by fraud to an imbecile, who cures him as well as restores his property rights. The film was re-made as *Bahurani* (Daughter-in-law) in a box-office-orientated form. Substitute love by a woman to cure a man's lunacy has been another cliche device used in *Khamoshi* (Silence) and *Khilauna* (Toy), both films of the 1970s. The asylum itself is generally used as the setting for comedy sequences, with the bit players let loose to do any nonsense they can think up.

Most other abnormal creatures are also shown for pity or fun. Beggars and minstrels with some physical deformity have been there to sing popular songs, right from the New Theatres era of the blind actor K. C. Dey down to Devendra Goel's later films where begging songs like *Ek paisa de de* (Give me one paisa) have been hits. Other comic creatures are dwarfs, the hairless, the toothless and the recent obnoxious 'discovery' of the sexless. The traditional eunuchs who sing and dance at ceremonies for a few coins have now become junior artists after some big colour films highlighted them successfully.

Youth and student unrest have rarely been tackled except in regional films. The first film about this topic was Tapan Sinha's Bengali *Apan Jan* (Our own people), re-made in Hindi as Gulzar's *Mere Apne* in which quite a few angry young actors got their chance to become popular. Otherwise, the depiction of campus or youth life has largely been crude and laughable with overgrown stars trying to play students and the anti-establishment cry getting drowned in songs and dances. Drug addiction and contraband traffic were dealt with in a serious vein in *Naya Nasha* (New intoxication) and with the popular trappings in Ramanand Sagar's *Charas* (Drug) and Dev Anand's *Hare Rama Hare Krishna*, the latter popularising composer R. D. Burman's ditty *Dam maro dam* (Smoke away) and also giving a message against the dope and hippy cult. The message which the screen pairs gave was that drugs weren't needed for happiness and that the audience should sing instead.

Sex themes also are rare. Shantaram's film *Parbat Pe Apna Dera* (My abode on the hills), 1944, about an ascetic brought down to sea-level and drowning himself in debauchery after years of suppression was notable. Recently, Shantaram's *Chaani* (Squirrel) based on a novel, had a cross-breed rural lass becoming the object of men's lust as well as fury, which destroy her. Other themes of man-woman relationship as a conflict between flesh and spirit were tackled in Debaki Bose's *Nartaki* (Dancer), 1940, and Kidar Sharma's *Jogan* (Female renouncer), 1950, as well as his two versions of *Chitralekha*, 1941 and 1964, about an old-world courtesan who caused tremors in the life of two men. P. C. Barua, a former prince and later a famed director under New Theatres in the 1930s, showed an obsession for this theme, in deep-thought films, *Mukti* (Freedom) about a painter marrying a high society girl who wants to divorce him and *Zindagi* (Life) about a male and a female drop-out, who try to live together platonically.

A poignant Bengali novel which has been filmed more than once is *Sahib, Bibi Aur Ghulam*, (Master, mistress, slave) about a strong-willed, lower-class girl married into a decaying feudal family who wants her wanton husband, even at the cost of becoming an alcoholic. Meena Kumari played the role in Guru Dutt's sensitive and technically brilliant Hindi adaptation. Earlier, he had made a comedy, *Mr. & Mrs. '55*, about an unemployed man taking on a rich pretty damsel, with an agreement of marriage and divorce on demand, and then winning her heart. In the 1970s a variation on the sexual topic took a rather crude and shocking form as sex-education films *Gupt Gyan, Gupt Shastra, Kaam Shastra* (All meaning private or sex knowledge) and *Stree Purush* (Man-woman). Under the cover of education along with Adults Only certificates, they showed as well as talked about hitherto taboo matters. They were seen by large numbers, had dubbed versions in other languages and have been banned and passed by turns over the last few years. And to think that it had been also done way back in 1929. The Social Purity League gave free shows for adults about what it called 'social evil', meant to save youths from ignorance. And Educational Pictures *Goharjaan* (name) made by H. R. Doctor showed a member of the Social Purity League going into a brothel and spearheading reforms about prostitution and its attendant dangers. Mr. Doctor said in his introduction that his attempt to show the inside view brought on him 'the mighty cut of the Bombay Board of Film Censor'.

Economic problems affecting the people are endemic, but they are too real and close to get a fully-fledged screen treatment. The usual argument is that people are fed up with the difficulties they face and in the cinema they want to 'escape' from their worries. So day to day problems or more grave matters are given a sweet icing of songs, choreographed numbers and comedy sequences. Only rarely is this effectively done, as in Gemini's *Mr. Sampat*, 1952, or Raj Kapoor's *Shri 420*, 1955, with satire as the medium.

The noted socialist writer and film maker K. A. Abbas, who also wrote

for many successful films of Raj Kapoor, has popularised two broad types of themes, blood versus upbringing and the poor man's search for the needs of life. The first took a spectacular form in Raj Kapoor's hit *Awara*, which said that the son of a judge can grow into a vagabond if he is socially despised and discarded. It is the environment which makes the man, whatever be the accident of birth or heredity. The theme has also shown brothers and sisters with contrary temperaments, as in Barua's *Adhikar* (Rights), 1938, and Abbas' own *Anhonee* (The impossible), 1952, later cheapened by the double-role dramas, which became commonplace.

Acute social problems were also highlighted in a grim fashion during the early 1950s with poverty as the common factor. Deprivation, suffering, disease and want among the poor or lower middle classes were to be seen in *Humlog* (We folks), 1951, *Boot Polish*, 1954, *Footpath*, 1953, *Awaz* (The cry), 1956, etc. but the trend did not last long. Abbas had heralded this raw and angry movement still earlier in 1946 with his *Dharti Ke Lal* (Children of the Earth). Taking the Bengal famine and the utter human degradation it caused, the film made a hard-hitting attack on many evils and the men behind them, though in a way which looks shrill in retrospect. The film sprang from theatrical roots — it was a cooperative effort by a left-wing troupe, the Indian People Theatre Association (IPTA), which was gaining strength with its new crop of ideas, artists, writers and craftsmen. Pandit Ravi Shankar contributed the film's music score. *Dharti Ke Lal* made an impact in other countries, especially the U.S.S.R., and Western critics also praised it with parts of it compared to Eisenstein at his best.

Also in 1946 Chetan Anand's *Neecha Nagar* (The town below) created an allegorical setting with the town higher up run by the land-owning despot and the one below led by an angry young man who also makes inroads into the heart of the rich man's daughter, finally bringing about the victory of the working class over the propertied. The film won one of the 11 Grand Prizes at the Cannes Festival.

A couple of years earlier, Bimal Roy under New Theatres had made two very powerful films, the Bengali *Udayer Pathey* (On the path of uplift) and its Hindi version *Humrahi* (Fellow travellers), which were unfortunately not sent abroad. The basic theme in the film, of upper and lower classes and the poor youth converting the rich man's daughter seemed the same. But it was given a radically different form, of an arrogant, self-respecting intellectual cum union leader pitted against a wealthy family, where the girl is transformed by his written works and her brother publishes them under his own name. The girl's gradual initiation into the life of the poor and her final split from her own class to join the youth formed a stronger plea for reform than any tub thumping. Songs were used sparsely and one of them was Tagore's *Jana gana mana* which later became India's national anthem (and was duly cut out from the film). Rich girl-poor boy stories have been filmed in their hundreds, but there is none to compare with Bimal Roy's film, except for a stray case (Mahesh Kaul's *Navjawan* [Youth], 1951), done in an ultra-light style.

The land owner and the tenant, the money lender and the victim, the capitalist employers and the working class have all been taken as the core of different films, but rarely with single-minded attention to the subject. Still, there were films which projected them sharply from the midst of other elements. In 1934, M. Bhavnani filmed a story by Premchand *The Mill* or *Mazdoor*, a telling depiction of the labour-capital inequality. The censors objected and the producers released it as 'the banned film' and one which carried the teachings of the national leaders. Sadly, Premchand himself was not happy with the film.

Mehboob's *Aurat* (Woman), 1940, starring his wife Sardar Akhtar was a big hit but it also brutally exposed some of the rampant evils of rural society which turned peasants into dacoits through the device of narrating the life of an average woman married into a farmer's family. In 1957, Mehboob re-made it with colour and grandeur as *Mother India* and it was nominated for an Oscar as best foreign-language film. Compared to the black and white original, however, the film sacrificed realism, especially in its excessive use of songs. Mehboob had made a stronger film 15 years earlier in *Roti* (Bread), a scorching indictment of the ruthless wealth-hoarding mentality and a call to the poor to snatch their rightful due, *Roti* showed the transformation of a tramp into a heartless capitalist. A recent film, Hrishikesh Mukherji's *Namak Haraam* (Ungrateful) used the unusual idea of two male friends, the poor one first helping the rich in suppressing the workers, then being converted to their side and dying. Pop stars Amitabh Bachchan and Rajesh Khanna played the two roles.

Films about the money lender's and landlord's exploitation of the helpless, illiterate and simple people, especially in villages, have taken various shapes. In 1925 Baburao Painter made the silent film *Savkari Pash* (Indian Shylock) and later re-made it in Marathi. In *Aurat*, this exploitation was a crucial part of the drama. But this theme's greatest expression occurred when Bimal Roy made *Do Bigha Zamin* (Two Acres of Land) in 1953. The film adopted the Italian neo-realistic style and used little-known actors such as Balraj Sahni as well as shooting mostly on village and city locations (well mixed with some studio work). But it also had a markedly Indian flavour and sowed the seeds of the humanist cinema in India, despite some big slices of melodrama, which stand out now after the film has dated. The lone peasant's struggle to save his land within three months, from the clutches of the zamindar who wants to build a factory, his vain appeal to law and justice, his journey to Calcutta to try to earn the money, but his decline into a beast of burden as a rickshaw-puller and his ultimate failure in the unequal fight all cried out for a curb on the socio-economic ills and a change in the existing order with of course a leftist solution suggested as the cure. The film created a stir in the complacent Hindi film world and it was awarded a prize at Cannes, yet at home it did only average business. Its innovation of realistic shooting, earthy acting and restricted use of four songs was barely followed up in the peculiar economic set-up of Hindi Cinema. When Bimal Roy made his next film on the acute problem of the educated unemployed he took recourse to comedy and songs, with comic singer-actor Kishore Kumar as the main player of the film called *Naukri*.

Like land, housing as another basic necessity and the desperate search for it, has led to noteworthy films such as Abbas' *Shaher Aur Sapna* and some new-wave films, discussed elsewhere in the book. But on a popular or melodramatic level, it has become a crutch for comedy, romance or

opposite top
In 1951 Raj Kapoor directed *Awara* which was a big draw in the Soviet Union.

opposite centre
Anhonee, 1952, was a well-crafted double-role drama with Nargis playing both good and bad sisters.

opposite bottom
Dharti Ke Lal, 1946, was a hard-hitting film on the Bengal famine and was acclaimed abroad.

below left
In 1934 M. Bhavnani filmed *The Mill* which was immediately banned by the censors.

below
Mother India which was nominated for an Oscar as best foreign-language film.

Savkari Pash, 1925, was one of the earliest realistic films to be made and concerned a young farmer at grips with a money lender.

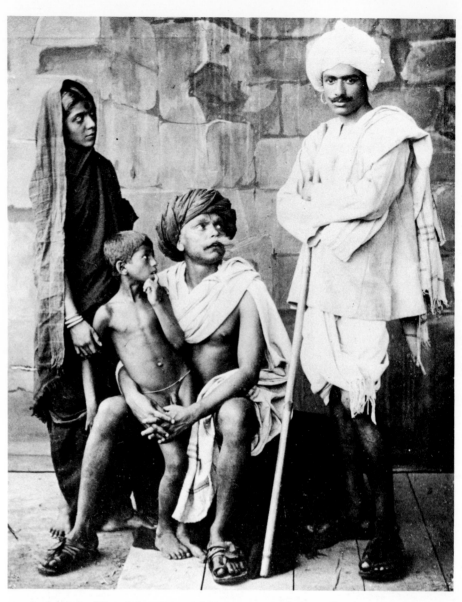

tearjerkers in films like *Pugree* (Premium paid for a flat), *Miss Mary* and *Anokhi Raat* (Strange night). Feudal aristocracy on the decline has been used for the old-new, rich-poor conflict in Abbas' *Aasmaan Mahal* (The sky palace) and Sohrab Modi's *Sheesh Mahal* (The glass palace).

There have also been exposé films. The independent journalist's fight against vested interests was dramatically shown in Bombay Talkies' *Naya Sangar* (New society), 1941, written by K. A. Abbas, then a pressman himself. Raj Kapoor's landmark achievement *Jagte Raho* (Be alert) in 1956 which won the top award from Karlovy Vary concerned a naive yokel's unintended unmasking of the respectable but anti-social people living in a large colony.

Many of the above leftist-slanted films have had the advantage of gaining markets in the socialist republics. The popularity of Raj Kapoor and his *Awara* [*Brodiyaga* in Russian] in the Soviet Union has been a phenomenon glowingly described in the Indian film press. These films have made a dent in non-Indian markets, created an off-beat cinema, made a plea for reform and, perhaps, stirred some consciences. However, all these attempts are pushed into the background when we come to the advent of Satyajit Ray as India's most uncompromising, steadfast and internationally-honoured film maker. His body of work from the Apu trilogy to *Chess Players* has covered all the problems discussed above and more, with a unique, subtle style that gives it a universal stature at a level higher than has been scaled until now. A more detailed discussion of his films can be found elsewhere in the book.

Indian Cinema has never been politically-conscious, producing instead light entertainment to help the audiences forget their cares. By 'politics' is not meant films about the freedom struggle in all its aspects, which are discussed elsewhere in the book, but an alertness for contemporary happenings and policies and a desire to probe or expose them, either satirically or seriously.

The problem of religion versus politics found its outlet in V. Shantaram's remarkable *Amrit Manthan*, 1934, about a dogmatic head priest at grips with the rulers. The film, a big hit in India, also took part in the Vienna Arts Exhibition.

Writer P. K. Atre and director-actor Master Winayak came together in the late 1930s to promote screen satire with political undercurrent in the Hindi-Marathi bilinguals: *Brahmachari* (on celibacy as a fad), *Brandy Ki Bottle* (on prohibition), *Dharamveer* (on hypocrisy). In later films, other directors made veiled attempts to caricature politicians, give an allegorical cloak to real developments or lampoon election tactics and other foibles of bureaucracy and administration. In two Hindi films of the 1970s the emphasis was very obvious. Gulzar's *Aandhi* (Storm) modelled its central female character on Mrs. Indira Gandhi; one song rather pungently attacked the plans and policies of her regime as she comes to attend an election meeting. The film was officially withdrawn during the Emergency period and later released with some cuts but the song remained intact. However, the most controversial film of the 1970s was *Kissa Kursi Ka* (The saga of the chair) made by politician and M.P. Amrit Nahata as a direct attack on the party in power. Its original unseen version, directed by Shivendra Sinha, was allegedly seized and burnt in its entirety during the Emergency, leading to court cases and furore after furore. Nahata re-made it scene by scene, again facing fresh problems and cuts by the censor under the new Janata regime. When released at last, the film was found to be crude and brazen by the intelligentsia and proved an immense flop. *Kissa* was really not worth burning.

Do Bigha Zamin, 1953, concerned the struggle between a peasant and his landlord which ended in the destruction of the former.

The Star System

Patience Cooper was one of the first true female stars of the silent era.

Deep-rooted in the Indian tradition is idol worship and guru worship, two sides of the same coin. While idolatry comes from religion and is directed at a superhuman entity, the guru cult extends to a leader, swami, teacher or any 'superior' being who does something which others cannot and who provides a figure from whom to seek solutions. He is usually a man, but exceptionally there is a female of the species, too.

Hero worship of film stars can be traced to these two streams. They are either the gods and goddesses, who achieve the impossible or alternatively they are attractive, wise, brave and lovable creatures who offer a model worthy of adoration and imitation. The guru image is one reason why those actors who play heroes in the different regional films apart from Hindi have been around for decades and have appeared in dozens of films (some of them are even addressed by that title). But actresses are more ephemeral; those who once played the heroes' sweethearts are now playing their mothers and aunts.

The craze for the most popular stars is disproportionate though also fickle. The star currently in the limelight becomes the image of people's longings; he (or she) is what they are not, but want to be. Take the exact opposite of all that the Indian stars stand for and it will apply to the common people. For instance, the 'angry young man', a popular image acted by Amitabh Bachchan, shows in reverse thousands of young men who cannot afford to be angry. Qualities and accomplishments are also admired in the star images, though people fully realise that they are not really the stars' own just as the make-up and singing voices are false. The illusion is all important for the time it lasts. When the effect wears off, a fresh ticket can buy another capsule of glamour and entertainment.

Inevitably, the result has been the creation of a star system in which it is the set-up that is to blame and not the stars. In the silent and early sound eras, the studios and big banners had the artists on their staff and lent them out occasionally 'by courtesy'. Then actors realised their drawing-power and plunged into indiscriminate freelancing. As the basically speculative nature of the industry slowly degenerated into a virtual gamble on every venture, films began to be bought and sold on names, primarily star names. Hence, all the chaos of Himalayan star fees, shooting time doled out by the hour in multiple shifts, unlimited contracts for the most popular actors, flops resulting in bankruptcy and the current trend to films with several stars which may be more likely to succeed, but is disastrous if they fail.

There have been many stars since feature films began in 1912-13. After the unknown heroes of the mythologicals laid down the norms of truth, goodness and moral strength, the more handsome and agile ones stepped in to play the popular heroes in Bombay-made films. The earliest with a semblance of star status was Khalil, a popular actor of several silent and some talkie films; another was Raja Sandow. In Bengal, Dhiren Ganguly was a comedy hero. Down South there were Y. V. Rao, T. P. Kailasam and one called Battling Mani. But the typical screen hero with his own aura and glamour emerged in Bombay in Master Vithal, who was titled 'India's Douglas Fairbanks'. Like many other stars of the silent screen, his downfall was the talkie as he could not speak dialogue. Taken as the hero of the first talkie *Alam Ara*, he was cast as a prince who remains in a trance for most of the picture. Other silent heroes who did succeed in sound were the Bilimoria brothers (D. and E.) Jal Merchant and Madhav Kale, while some of the newer faces were Prithviraj Kapoor, P. Jairaj and Mubarak. They had tough competition from the singing-speaking stage professionals who were immediately in much demand as the early talkies were simply filmed stageplays; the top name among them was Master Nissar, who was paired with singer actress Jahan Ara Kajjan and made some of the biggest musical hits in 1931-34, for Madan Theatres.

Film maker V. Shantaram, who had acted in silents, again became a lead player for his own movies and continued for many years as did Sohrab Modi. In New Theatres, the only director-star was Barua, who brought in a casual relaxed style in some memorable roles in Bengali-Hindi films. The steadier professional actors emerged with Ashok Kumar in 1936. He has had the longest spell down to films of 1979, but with all sorts of roles in all sorts of films. Jairaj is another who has had a long innings of fifty years as actor. Others of that period were Motilal, jovial and lovable and Surendra, tall, rugged and a melodious singer.

But one who really touched the skies was K. L. Saigal, a natural actor, but more than that, a singer with a magic voice that has never found its match. His songs have made him a legend, though he died prematurely. Some like Yakub, Jagirdar, Jayant and Chandramohan were versatile, while others including Pagnis ('Tukaram') and Radhamohan Bhattacharya ('Humrahi') were one-film heroes who left a mark. Prithviraj, tall and Grecian, brought an imposing aura to his roles as well as managing a Hindi theatre troupe which brought new talents to the cinema including his own sons Raj, Shammi and Shashi. Since Raj's sons Randhir and Rishi have also become popular heroes and others are on their way, the Kapoors have indeed spread like a banyan tree in films.

above
Khalil was the first male star of the silent era.

left
Sulochna (Ruby Mayers) was one of the most glamorous heroines of the silent screen.

71

above
Prithviraj Kapoor began in silent films, but was also successful in talking pictures as were his sons, Raj, Shammi and Shashi.

right
Jahan Ara Kajjan was a leading singer in musicals from 1931 to 1935.

below
Dilip Kumar was one of the top three stars from 1946 onwards.

opposite
Madhubala was an actress who displayed great magnetism in her performances in the 1940s and 1950s.

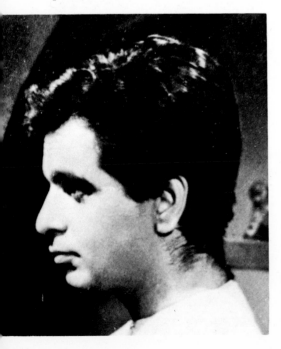

Raj Kapoor, Dilip Kumar and Dev Anand were the trio which dominated the hero image for almost a quarter century from the late 1940s. They were the idols of a new generation — Dilip the tragedian, Raj the tragicomic and Dev the debonair, taking life and love as they came. These stars no doubt developed their own styles and mannerisms, but they were at least distinct actors, unlike the new crop that was to follow them. Two contemporaries, Guru Dutt and Balraj Sahni, were less popular, but still good actors. No less well-liked in their own way have been the second-line heroes Premnath and Rehman, villains from Pran down to Prem Chopra, comedians from Dixit and Gope to Johnny Walker and Mehmood, child stars from Vasanti, Daisy, Honey and Naaz down to Master Raju and the stunt actors from the Pahelwans (musclemen) of the silent era, John Cawas, Boman Shroff up to Dara Singh the mat-man of today.

Some new trends in the late 1950s created new heroes in Shammi Kapoor (a virile vigorous image), Raaj Kumar, Rajendra Kumar, Shashi Kapoor, Sunil Dutt and others. In the last two decades, we have had a good number of marquee names in Dharmendra, Manoj Kumar, Feroz Khan, Sanjay, Jeetendra, Rajesh Khanna, Shatrughan Sinha, Vinod

clockwise from top
Suchitra Sen was Bengal's top heroine
for many years; Suraiya; Nalini
Jaywant.

below
Balraj Sahni

Khanna, Sachin, Amol Palekar and Mithun Chakravarty. Amitabh Bachchan enjoyed phenomenal success from 1976-77 and Sanjeev Kumar displayed a great deal of versatility as a star actor. The regions have had their own big names sprawled over the decades led by M. G. R. who used cinema for political objectives and ultimately became the Chief Minister of Tamil Nadu. In Tamil there are Shivaji Ganesan, Gemini Ganesh and others, Raj Kumar in Kannada, Prem Nazir and Madhu in Malayalam, A. Nageswar Rao and N. T. Rama Rao in Telugu, with Kamalahasan shuttling successfully between all four. Bengal has its matinee idol in Uttam Kumar followed by Soumitra Chatterji, who has acted in 10 films of Satyajit Ray, a unique honour.

On the female side, among the earliest stars after Phalke's little girl Mandakini was Patience Cooper, a consistent star name of Madan Theatres all through the silents. Sita Devi, also an Anglo-Indian, followed with Himansu Rai's films to back her. An actress who dared to become a producer-director around 1925 was Fatma Begum. She also had stars in the house in her three pretty daughters: Sultana, Shahzadi and Zubeida (the last became the heroine of the first talkie). Bangalore even had its own 'Garbo' sisters, Wilma and Jena, however, the true silent era star was Sulochna (Ruby Mayers) of the Imperial banner.

The heroines created by the talkie were primarily singers: Calcutta's

Jahan Ara Kajjan, Bombay's Jaddanbai (who also made films and composed music), Durga Khote, Shanta Apte, Kanan Devi, Jamuna and Chhaya Devi. Devika Rani in Himansu Rai's Bombay Talkies soon became the 'screen's first lady' of her time, also winning international renown.

This was the heyday for singing stars Khurshid, Nurjehan (later citizens of Pakistan) and then Suraiya who achieved great personal fame. Naseem, Begum Para, Rehana, Shobhna Samarth, Snehprabha were big names in the 1930s to be replaced by Nargis, Nalini Jaywant, Madhubala, Kamini Kaushal and Geeta Bali. The South has had its Bhanumati (also a film maker), Anjali Devi, Savitri, B. Saroja Devi, Kalpana, Sharda and Sheela. And Bengal loved its Suchitra Sen, followed by Sandhya Roy, Arundhati Devi, Manju Dey and then Aparna Sen and Madhabi Mukherji.

The next crop had some other gifted actresses: Meena Kumari, Nutan, Nimmi, Usha Kiron, Nanda, Tanuja, followed by Mala Sinha, Waheeda Rehman, Sandhya, the more mod and youthful type—Asha Parekh and Sadhana in the 1960s down to recent ones like Sharmila Tagore (a Ray discovery becoming an all-India star), Mumtaz, Saira Banu, Simi, Raakhee, Rekha, Zeenat Aman, Parveen Babi, Reena Roy, Moushumi, Sarika, Ranjeeta, Helen, Padma Khanna and Komilla Wirk. While most of them lean on glamour and exposure, the histrionic flame has been kept flickering, however desperately, by Jaya Bhaduri, Shabana Azmi, Simi, Rehana Sultan, Smita Patil, Sharmila, Rakhee and a few others.

The star system was never so dubious as in the 1970s. An ever-increasing number of mediocre producers keep entering the film industry and hitching their wagons to stars with scant regard for the films' quality. Professionalism has badly declined as erratic behaviour by some stars and other monopoly talents in singing or composing is taken

top to bottom
Zubeida, another popular silent star and heroine of the first talkie; Sharmila Tagore; Bengali actress Sandhya Roy.

left
Sanjeev Kumar

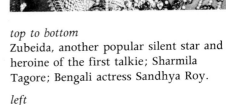

above left and above right
Ashok Kumar, known as the evergreen actor, has appeared in over 200 films; Raj Kapoor.

below
Kishore Kumar, a top playback singer and comic actor.

for granted. The worst role is played by the media, especially the seductively printed film magazines which are just like the films — attractive in appearance, shallow in content. Their promotion of the stars, with numberless photos and stories having a tie-up with the new releases, act as the biggest supporter of the system. There are about 600 film publications, but only a few write sensibly about cinema itself.

Cheap gossip, brazenly written and bordering on porn, is rammed down the throats of readers. Justifications for it sound exactly like the argument of the commercialised producer: 'We give cabaret, rape and violence because people want it'. Gossip is fallaciously made out to be a weapon to keep the stars in their place yet actually it puts them in a much better bargaining position with all the attractive photos much more important than the written word. With the rate of literacy moderate and the reading habit corroded by other factors, it is obvious that the magazines are mostly 'seen' and not 'read'. Sometimes, stars feed the scandal machine for the sake of their films, having heavy financial stakes and often being disguised producers or distributors. At times it is done to spite rivals, often it is resented and there have been instances of reporters being threatened or beaten.

Mr. B. K. Karanjia, who has been editor of two top publications, the fortnightly *Filmfare* and the trade weekly *Screen*, explains the tangle with the following arguments: 'Gossip in film magazines affects the stars but hardly ever the star system. The system is strong for so many years because pictures are sold on the names of leading stars. Because of their importance they have on occasions hampered the work of the director. In normal life, they are friendly and interesting people, interested in the betterment of films but finding themselves in a vicious circle. Because of the uncertainties of film-making, several pictures started are not completed. So they are tempted to sign up as many films as possible'. About journalism Mr. Karanjia says from his long experience: 'Star orientation in journalism has led to further deterioration of our cinema's quality. Film criticism in the real sense is sadly lacking. The functions of film publications should be to guide readers and provide honest criticism. There is certainly an audience for film magazines not merely dwelling on stars. The difficulty is that there is seldom finance available for such magazines'.

As it stands, the stars are in a very dominant position, more so the males, with everything about the film tailored to suit them. In an attempt to obtain the handful of popular stars who sell, even the human element is forgotten. If they fall sick or are unable to work for some time the entire industry and its economy are shaken up. And two or three successive flops sharply decrease the star's value. Stars are also confident that their personal lives seldom affect the star image, like a scandal, a marriage, a political affiliation or an income tax raid. If the screen illusion is well built up, everything else is forgotten. More than a decade ago, income tax checks on the houses of some personalities brought forth a cool twenty lakhs from the bathroom of an actress. A loyal film publication, compelled to give the news, supported it with a prominent item stating that the film people concerned gave the fullest possible co-operation to the officers. Soon after, the actress appeared in a patriotic role in a successful film and won a lot of applause for her work.

top
Bhanumati, a star from the South.

above
Shabana Azmi

left
Waheeda Rehman, a talented, sensitive actress of the 1960s.

77

Many Regions, Many Tongues

The diversity of India's regions, languages and ways of life came to the surface as soon as talking pictures began. It was evident that within a general mainstream of culture, there were several sub-cultures also crying out for expression. The folk and art forms were already there, but cinema was an exciting new sphere where a province could widely speak and hear its own tongue and perhaps also get it heard by others.

This desire to make and see films in one's own language as against the commonly understood Hindi must have been so strong that from 1931 until today some 8000 films have been made in as many as 30 regional languages and dialects. But the regional film has also brought up its built-in dilemma of limited budgets and markets. If films could be artistic and realistic, they have also to be modest. The Hindi film with all-India and foreign traditional markets could treat subjects properly, but usually in an inevitably vulgarised, commercialised form. This conflict has come right down to the recent 'new cinema' in India, in which regional films have been playing a big role.

The early years were marked more by the novelty of hearing a new language in the new sound medium than by dramatic reasons. So, soon after *Alam Ara* there was a babel of tongues on the screen, with three regional language films in the very first talkie year and four more within the following two.

It is best to divide the regional films into three main zones and it must also be admitted that it is physically impossible for any single observer or critic, however sharp his eye, to view the whole output of Indian Cinema. Apart from the bulk (nearly 400 regional films each year), there is the inevitable bar of language and distance. It would need a brave soul, indeed, to keep hopping between different centres and seeing all the films, that too with an interpreter by the side. The three zones on the basis of production, include the Eastern (having Bengali, Assamese, Oriya), the Southern (with Tamil, Telugu, Malayalam, Kannada and Tulu) and the Western (including Marathi, Gujarati, Konkani, Punjabi, Haryanvi, Sindhi, Rajasthani, Dogri, Kashmiri, Coorgi, Manipuri, Bhojpuri, Avadhi, Maithili, Chhatisgarhi and Magadhi). The zones were once broadly represented by Calcutta, Madras with Hyderabad and Bombay, but in recent years, production centres have sprung up in Assam, Karnataka, Kerala, Gujarat and the Punjab.

Apart from above languages, India has also made films in English (in addition to English versions or co-productions), Nepali, Persian, German, Sinhalese, Arabic and Pushtu. Of course, these are a very small number made at many different times.

Bengali The most prominent in the Eastern circuit is of course the Bengali Cinema, made more glorious on a world scale by Satyajit Ray's films. It wasn't surprising that in other countries, Bengali cinema was identified as Indian cinema until recently.

Bengal has had an artistic, literary, cultural and intellectual tradition which has not been affected by the prevailing adversity. Even now, it is heart-warming to see the simple austere way in which a director of Ray's

Grihadaha was a 1936 Bengali film directed by Barua.

calibre has to work and the many practical problems and technical handicaps he overcomes day by day. He calls it a challenge for being more inventive and economical, loves to work there alone, but wishes that the conditions were better.

An account of Ray's films can be found in the final chapter. So too, the more 'nouvelle' works of Mrinal Sen, Ritwik Ghatak and some recent film makers in other regional languages. Surveying the Bengali film scene, before and after Ray's arrival, we find that this regional cinema was more enlightened and evolutionary than others even in the 'silent' period. Literary masterpieces were selected and filmed at that early stage and Madan Theatres' *Kapal Kundala* based on Bankim Chandra's novel became the first film to run for 25 weeks (in Calcutta). Directors with a natural gift and an intelligent resistance to cliches have kept the Bengali Cinema always some steps ahead of the others, supported, of course, by a more discriminating audience.

The first Bengali talkie was *Jamai Sasthi*, a comedy directed by Amar Choudhry which came just a month after *Alam Ara*. The rich formative period was nursed by B. N. Sircar's legendary institution New Theatres and the landmarks created by its directors: Debaki Bose, Nitin Bose, Hemchander, Phani Mazumdar and Barua. These laid the foundations and Bengali films continued the tradition with films of some literary-lyrical-cultural merit, though not completely free from popular elements of screen entertainment and having an overall conventional format.

An average of 40 films each year has normally been produced, though it varies with the ups and downs this cinema has faced, the biggest blow being the loss of the East Bengal market after the country's partition.

above
A 1967 remake of *Grihadaha* with Bengal's top pair Uttam Kumar (left) and Suchitra Sen.

above right
Haatey Bazarey was another Bengali film which also appeared in 1967.

A scene from *Valli Kalyanam*, one of the earliest Tamil films to be made.

Themes with a modern social background and a maudlin base are the commonest, apart from those adapted from Tagore, Bankim or Sarat Chandra and the biographical films. Among the directors who have won a large reputation are Mrinal Sen, Tapan Sinha, Ritwik Ghatak, Tarun Majumdar, Ajoy Kar, Rajen Tarafdar, Purnendu Patrea, Asit Sen and some others. In all, about 1500 Bengali films have been made to date.

Assamese and Oriya One of the tiniest among the long established regional cinemas is the Assamese, with a total output of some 80 films till now. The first film was made in that picturesque region in 1933 by Jyotiprasad Agarwala. Called *Joymati*, it was a historical drama. Another film from this pioneer came four years later since when there has been intermittent production. Some of the noted directors are Bhupen Hazarika, Prabhat Mukherji, Abdul Mazid, Bhaben Saikia. Most films were produced in Calcutta, but recently a studio has been promoted in Gauhati by the state government.

Even smaller is the contribution of Orissa with about 65 films since the first was made in 1936. (It was a mythological titled *Sitar Bibah* and produced by Kali Films.) Modern directors with good productions to their credit include Ghanshyam Mahapatra and Biplab Rai Chaundhry.

Tamil The South with its four major languages cumulatively accounts for about 5000 of the 8000 regional films and at present about 60% of the total annual output. Inter-dubbing among the languages is also quite common. The most prolific of its four languages is Tamil with over 2000 films to date. The first, *Kalidasa*, was made in 1931 in Bombay and was another pioneering venture of Ardeshir Irani's Imperial Company with singer-actress T. P. Rajalakshmi in the cast. Early Tamil films were also made by other Bombay and Calcutta companies until Madras developed as a talkie production centre and gradually became the most flourishing and organised, with other Southern language films also produced there. Madras now has some of the biggest and most systematically-run film studios in India.

Most of the Tamil films resemble Hindi ones, being three hours long and full of songs, dances, comedy and spectacle but are different in their concentration upon mythology, folklore and fantasy as well as a heavy theatrical bias in filming and acting. But an aspect for which the Tamil cinema remains unique in India is the political base given by active party workers who have been screenplay and dialogue writers, lyricists,

leading actors and film makers. The D.M.K. ideology was so much popularised through some films and their components that it brought the party to power.

Of course, the spearheading was done by a glamorous screen hero, commanding all the worship of the masses. M.G.R., or M. G. Ramachandran, acted in scores of hit films all of which had some political slant.

top
The Tamil film *Saraswati Sabadam* with Sivaji Ganesan.

above left and above
M.G.R. interrogates Ranga Rao, and also in *Naam Nadu*.

above
Smita Patil, a talented modern actress, in *Gaman* as a village wife sustaining herself on the letters of her husband who has migrated to the city.

right
Safed Haathi was a recent children's film about a boy and a white elephant.

opposite top
Koshish showed the problems of a deaf and dumb couple played by Jaya Bhaduri as the mother and Sanjeev Kumar as the father.

opposite bottom
Santaan showed Nirupa Roy as a typical domesticated woman happy to be 'trapped' in the kitchen.

Theerpu (Judgement), a Telugu film starring N. T. Rama Rao.

below
The Malayalam film *Kodiyettom*.

below right
Another Malayalam film, *Swapnam*.

When there was a split in the party and M. G. R. formed his own, the magnetic pull of his own personality stood out, as his group came to power and he became the Chief Minister of Tamil Nadu. Whether he should still continue to act in films having achieved that position, was a subject of hot debate and even a couple of law suits.

Interaction between Madras and Bombay has led to the South's Cinema regularly distributing its films throughout India. It started with S. S. Vasan of Gemini Studio dubbing his extravaganza *Chandralekha* (1948) in Hindi and capturing the whole Indian market in a big way. Ever since then Madras producers have been tapping Bombay's talents in acting, writing and music and their own in the technical branches to make large and successful Hindi films which are clever re-makes of hits in South Indian languages. This trend declined some time back and recently reversed itself with the South re-making Hindi films. Either way it has led to an exchange of talent with many of South's gifted actors becoming famous throughout India. The only difference in the films is that when a Tamil film is made into Hindi, the political slant is nowhere to be found.

Telugu The regional cinema of Andhra Pradesh also had an early start when *Bhakta Prahalad*, a mythological, was made in the first talkie year in Bombay by H. M. Reddi. It was a production of Bharat Movietone and was made at the Krishnatone Studio which was also in the race for the first talkie feature. Similar films were made in Bombay-Calcutta with the help of Telugu troupes.

Since then, about 1700 films have been made at Madras, Hyderabad-Secunderabad and elsewhere with the annual output reaching the highest figure recently among South's languages. Telugu cinema also follows the Tamil and Hindi models. Since it commands a fairly numerous and receptive audience, it can create spectacular productions in colour and 'scope processes just like Tamil. Bilinguals in the two tongues have also been common, like Hindi-Bengali from Calcutta and Hindi-Marathi from Bombay. Re-making in Hindi has also been done with some Telugu artists. The state government's massive subsidies and other aids have propped up Andhra as an important production base.

Malayalam Starting a little late in 1938, the regional cinema of Kerala (mostly functioning in Madras until the 1970s) has made big strides recently, with 90-120 films each year, about 900 in total, and studios becoming more active in the state itself. The first film, *Balan*, was made by Modern Theatres. After a few efforts and a long gap, this regional cinema was established after 1952. Recently, with new prosperity coming from the emigrants to the Gulf countries, production has boomed, and a variety of themes have been tried out including those about sex.

Still the small market, the low budget and the literate, intelligent audience has led to the blooming of an artistic, realistic, off-beat cinema

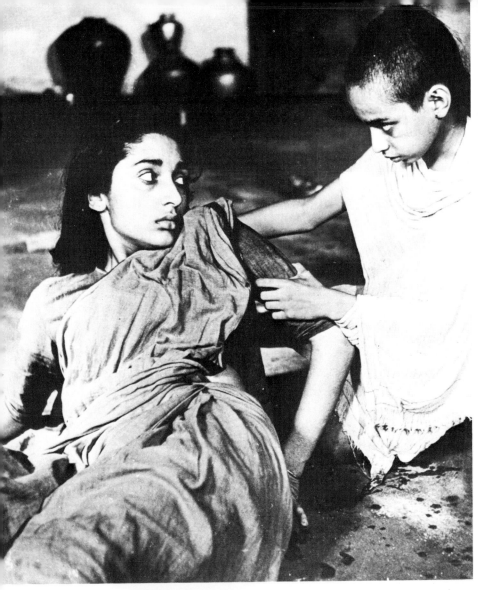

above left
Ghatashraddha, 1977, is the most recent
film from Kannada to win the top
national film award. Its cast included
Meena (left) and Ajit Kumar.

above
Nirmalyam was a Malayalam award-
winner produced in 1973.

left
Mukti (Deliverance) was a feature film
from Kannada on the influence of
parental sins on their innocent children.
The young lovers were played by Raj
Shekhar (left) and Kalpana.

rooted in the region. It has also been one of the leading contributors to
the Indian 'new cinema' which, like Kannada, finds a place in the
concluding chapter. The striking point is that even in its popular format,
the Malayalam Cinema has not taken to the kind of gaudy spectacles
found in Tamil, Telugu and Hindi, but has preferred to stick to the
literature and ethos of its own province.

Kannada This regional cinema of Karnataka (Mysore) at first produced
typical films about legends and folklore. The first film, *Dhruva Kumar*, a
mythological, was made in 1934 by Jayawani Talkies in Bombay. Later,
centralised in Madras, it slowly grew within the state itself, with studios
at Bangalore and Mysore. Recent boosts by the state government has sent

overleaf
A scene from *Charas* portraying a drug-
induced hallucination.

The Marathi film industry received a big boost with *Sant Tukaram*, 1936, a devotional film starring V. Pagnis.

right
Amar Bhoopali was a Marathi biography of the famous poet.

below
Seema in a very popular pin-up pose for the Malayalam film *Her Nights* which was a big South Indian hit.

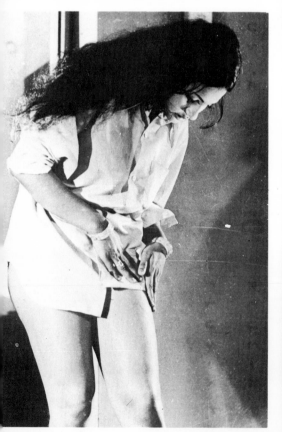

the production spiralling from five to 50 a year with about 700 films completed to date. A fresh resurgence in quality has also come with many socially topical subjects being treated in an avant-garde style.

Films have also been made in the minor dialects of Tulu and Coorgi, although not many. There have been only a couple of Tulu films made each year from 1971 onwards, while the lone Coorgi film (*Nada Manne Nada Koolu*) came in 1972.

Marathi In the Western zone the oldest and also the most known is the Marathi cinema. Since the Prabhat Film Co. of Kolhapur with V. Shantaram as the presiding partner had a natural Marathi base, the first film in the language emerged from it in 1932, along with a Hindi counterpart for the all-India audience.

It was *Ayodhyecha Raja* or *King of Ayodhya* directed by Shantaram and based on Phalke's trusted old tale of Raja Harishchandra, featuring singer-actor G. Tembe with Durga Khote. The Marathi-orientated films, like Bengali or Gujarati, date back still further to the silent era, since many films made and performed by talents of the region were markedly provincial in their costume, custom and culture. To state a contradiction in terms, they can be called silent Marathi films, with only the sub-titles on the cards being in English and Hindi. After the coming of sound, the Marathi film took its own shape and its hour of glory was soon reached in the 1936 *Sant Tukaram*, declared one of the three best films at the Venice Film Festival.

Only about 600 Marathi films have been made. By way of quality, the Marathi industry kept up a good reputation of provincial realism and using literary themes, not unmixed with the popular aids of music and mushy melodrama. The hallmarks were either stark tragedy or biting

left
A folk-dance from the Marathi film
Jait Re Jait.

satire. It also banked on its typical folk form of the 'tamasha' with several films based on it, but in the last few years it has been corroded by the spectre of box office survival and the near-by model provided by the Bombay film in Hindi. It now has little individual identity, though there is immense scope for it.

Among its notable directors, before the decline, we can mention pioneer Baburao Painter, Bhal G. Pendharkar, Master Winayak, Damle and Fatehlal, G. Jagirdar, Vasant Joglekar, Datta Dharmadhikari, Raja Paranjpe, Ram Gabale, Raja Thakur, and Dinkar Patil. In the heyday, production activity had spread to Kolhapur and Poona, apart from Bombay. Now, there is little more than an occasional film made in Kolhapur and the routine quota from Bombay.

Gujarati The population of proper Bombay is divided into a large number of Marathi and Gujarati speaking people. So the silent films and the early talkie ones were also similarly divided. When Gujarati or Parsi film makers and actors were involved, the films took on a typical Gujarati ethos in the way the characters dressed and the life-style they adopted. Even the names of many films were given in Gujarati. A number of films were adapted straight from the Gujarati stage so that a peculiar theatricality stuck to this cinema and still persists.

The first talkie, *Narsinh Mehta* in 1932, was a devotional on the famous poet-saint and was produced by Chimanlal Desai and directed by Nanubhai Vakil. Other big companies including Chandulal Shah's Ranjit and Vijay-Shankar Bhatt's Prakash Pictures made their share, often through double-language versions with Hindi. Some important films such as *Achhoot* (Untouchable) had a predominantly Gujarati base with the Hindi version as the supplementary one. However, the production level could not be kept up for long because of the limited audience, which preferred to see Hindi films. In 1976, the annual production jumped to 30 and this number was also made in the following two years so that the total record now touches about 300 films. This spurt is due to the state government showing a sudden abundance of interest and providing subsidies, grants and exemptions. Studios and production offices have sprung up in Baroda and other places, though the standard has not substantially changed since the films cash in upon the same old

page 90 (left to right)
top: Neetu Singh, Rekha, Sharmila Tagore *centre:* Zeenat Aman, Vidya Sinha *bottom:* Sulakshana Pandit, Hema Malini, Shabana Azmi

page 91 (left to right)
top: Amitabh Bachchan, Rishi Kapoor, Dharmendra *centre:* Feroz Khan, Rajesh Khanna *bottom:* Manoj Kumar, Shashi Kapoor, Dev Anand

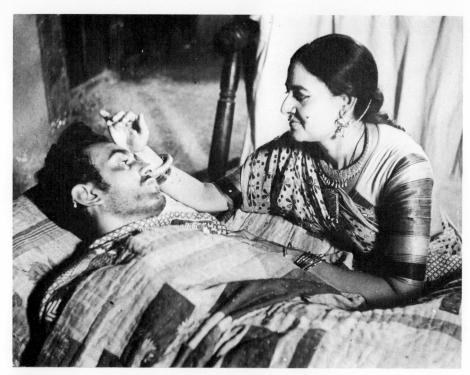

themes of myths, saint stories, folk lore and legends about kings or outlaws.

Among the popular directors in its brief history, we can mention V. M. Vyas, Nanabhai Bhatt, Dhirubhai Desai, Ratibhai Punatar, Chaturbhuj Doshi, Ramchandra Thakur, Manhar Raskapoor and recently Govind Saraiya, Kantilal Rathod and Feroz Sarkar. One benefit of the Gujarati stage cum screen tradition has been the discovery of excellent actors for the Hindi screen such as Sanjeev Kumar.

Punjabi Starting in 1935 with *Ishke Punjab* (Love for Punjab) this regional cinema has produced 150 films, some made in pre-Partition Punjab and most of the rest in Bombay. Based on love legends or broad comedies taken from the theatre, it is largely of poor quality. Surprisingly, many of the popular Bombay talents belong to this community but they have not thought it worthwhile to explore the region's possibilities for unusual types of films. A film based on Rajinder Singh Bedi's novel was started, but was left incomplete on the death of its producer, actress Geeta Bali.

Meanwhile, its sister state Haryana has also come up with two Haryanvi films in 1973 and 1974, the first being *Beera Shera* (Brave lion).

Bhojpuri and Other Dialects Bihar's spoken language Bhojpuri first appeared on screen in films in Hindi with which it has much similarity. Minor characters in Bombay films, for example milkmen or domestics, used to speak in this language so people were familiar with it. Then Dilip Kumar's hit *Ganga Jamna* in 1961 used Bhojpuri in most of its dialogue and some popular songs to spur the belated creation of the first Bhojpuri film, *Ganga Maiya Tohe Piyari Chadhaibo* (Offerings to Mother Ganges), in 1962. Directed by Kundan Kumar, the film was a typical romantic melodrama but the novelty of its language and folk music made it such a sensational hit that it let loose a flood of films in this and its sister dialects.

For a time, the industry had its Bhojpuri craze (like any other phase that succeeds by success). About 18 films were made up until 1966 and one Avadhi in 1964, two Chhatisgadhi after 1965 and two Magadhi in 1964-65. But the flow dried up as the novelty wore off and the audience shrank in markets already dominated by big Hindi films. For the record, *Goswami Tulsidas* was the first in Avadhi, *Kahi Debe Sandesh* (The message giving) in Chhatisgadhi, *Bhaiya* (Brother) in Magadhi and *Kanyadaan* (Daughter's marriage) in Maithili.

Sindhi   The first Sindhi film *Ekta* (Oneness) was made in 1942 by J. B. H. Wadia as a plea for intercommunal harmony, but there were no other Sindhi films for 16 years. Sindhi films have suffered because of its small audience scattered over various regions in two countries. Though the rich business community could support a worthwhile Sindhi cinema, it is more addicted to Hindi films and takes its own language films casually. Consequently, only about 15 films have been made, mostly of poor quality.

Rajasthani   The languages of Rajputana, Marwari and Rajasthani, have found an outlet in approximately a dozen films. The first was *Nazrana* (Gift) in 1942, directed by G. P. Kapoor. The second came after two decades, *Babasa Ri Ladli* made by Adarsh. Production has remained meagre in the last ten years.

Konkani   Another microscopic regional cinema, with only two films and two producers till the 1960s, Konkani films began with *Mogacho Aundo* in 1949 made by actor Al Jerry Braganza. The second film was *Amchem Noxib* produced by Frank Fernand and directed by A. Salam. A good effort, true to the language, was *Nirmon* by the same director in 1965; it was even remade in Hindi. Though Konkani has vast scope in its own particular background, it prefers to rely on the theatre for its sources in the dozen or so films made till now.

The first Sindhi film to be made was *Ekta* dealing with the problems of inter-communal unity.

A still from the first Rajasthani film, *Nazrana*.

right
Vasudeo Rao, a brilliant actor, as a
work-hating old villager in Mrinal Sen's
Telugu film *Oka Oorie Katha* (Story of a
village).

below
Ondanondu Kaladalli (Once upon a time)
is a Kannada film that is concerned
with the Samurai tradition in
Karnataka.

opposite
M. G. Ramachandran is both a famous
hero of Indian Cinema and Chief
Minister of Tamil Nadu state. Here he is
seen in *Enga Veetu Pillai*, a very
popular double-role drama in which he
plays two brothers of contrasting
temperaments.

Dukhtare Loor was an Iranian film made in 1933 by Ardeshir Irani.

Other Indian Languages Among others, with very tiny production figures, Manipuri has shown a recent spurt of half a dozen films from 1972 to 1979. There have been two Kashmiri films after 1964 and one Dogri in 1966. The first Manipuri film was *Matamgi Manipur*, the Kashmiri was *Mainz Raat* and the Dogri was *Gallan Hoian Beetian*.

Non-Indian Languages Films in English have numbered about 30 starting with *Nurjehan* in 1932 and also covering some films made in English alone, apart from the special versions and co-productions already discussed. *Pamposh* also had a German version. There were ten Indian-Iranian films starting in 1933 with *Dukhtare Loor* made by Ardeshir Irani as a novelty for exploring a new territory. Later some Hindi films were dubbed for tapping the Iran market. An Indo-Iran co-production *Subah-O-Sham* in the two languages fared badly in both. Two action films of Homi Wadia were dubbed into Arabic in 1943-44. A Sinhalese film *Broken Promise* was made in 1947. A Nepali film *Harishchandra* was produced in 1951 while another was *Maiti Ghar* with star Mala Sinha and her husband C. P. Lohani. *Laila Majnu* was made in Pushtu in 1941 by Sharad Productions of Bombay. A Thai film *Talash* was made in 1972.

And, after noting films in such a huge number of diverse tongues, one is still not sure what new surprise will be sprung by film makers. There are still languages and dialects left to be explored. But the crowning glory would be a film in Sanskrit, India's ancient root language. The trouble is there are hardly 500 people who understand it.

overleaf top
A regional folk-dance in the Tamil film
Mullum Malarum.

overleaf bottom
Chemmeen was a Malayalam film on the
lives of fisherfolk and featured Satyan
and Sheela.

overleaf opposite
Santu Rangili with Aruna Irani (right)
and Upendra Trivedi was a Gujarati
film based on George Bernard Shaw's
Pygmalion.

Palanka was a joint Indian-Bangladesh
co-production featuring Sandhya Roy
(left) and Anwar.

97

Censorship and the Government

Perhaps in no other country does the government have so much control of films as in India, for better or for worse. The laws, the levies and the organisations, (whether for development and aid or control and monopoly), now touch almost every aspect of the film industry.

The most debated and hated aspect of governmental control is censorship, enforced by the Cinematograph Act and executed by the Central Board of Film Censors and its officers with headquarters in Bombay and branches in Madras and Calcutta. There are a large number of honorary panel members and a few board members, but the practical system devised over the years is so foolproof that they are left with very little choice, whereas the actual censoring is done by the office staff.

The primary question is whether there can be film censorship at all when there is none on other equally potent media such as the press, drama and the novel. One argument is that in a country like India, with films reaching the widest possible and the most diversified audience and film makers not showing any particular sense of social responsibility, total freedom might lead to total chaos. Another belief is that cinema, like everything else, should be left under the common law.

If in principle film censorship is accepted, then ways and means have to be found to make it more consistent, logical and genuine. Most important is to give it a sense of direction so clear and well-conceived that both film makers and censors know where they stand with little scope left for misinterpretation.

In the pre-Independence years, censorship was mainly political. Direct or indirect depiction of or reference to national leaders, the struggle for freedom and any mass upsurge or fight against unjust rule were scrutinised very closely. (In one case *Mahatma* was changed to *Dharmatma* as the film was about a saint whose teachings about untouchability were the same as those of Mahatma Gandhi.) Censorship varied between provinces, leading to difficulties and incongruities; often people of one state enjoyed a film for weeks while others were prohibited from seeing it. The police also had a hand in censorship and in fact before the different boards emerged, the police commissioner's office used to grant permission. Later, too, a police representative was often included on the board of censors and the commissioner acted as an ex-officio president. Today ex-judges of law courts are appointed as jury chairmen for film awards, given away by many different organisations. The impression perhaps persists that film making is some sort of a crime.

The Cinematograph Act of 1918 created the provincial boards of censors and from 1952 came the Central Board system which has continued over the years. The highly confused nature of the code and its functioning can be surmised from the extreme reactions to censorship. One side, including those who administer it, consider it too conservative while others find it too liberal. The panel and board members are themselves selected from these two extremes with the result that uniformity is the first casualty. The reasonable compromise is surely to have clear, balanced guidelines implemented by level-headed members. Still funnier is the contradiction of one section of the film

A scene from *Buniyaad* that, surprisingly, was not censored.

A kiss in an early silent film *A Throw Of Dice* starring the Anglo-Indian actress Sita Devi and Charu Roy. The film was made in 1930 by Himansu Rai as a co-production with Britain and Germany.

industry attacking censorship as a curb on freedom while another prefers it as a protective measure. (If and when a film is legally prosecuted on any grounds, the certificate allowing the objected portions acts like a seal of official sanction.) Liberalisation has seldom been envisaged for the development of film art on newer themes.

Over a quarter of a century of this doublethink on censorship has led to a situation, stoically accepted, where some films face a lot of cuts and prolonged bans while similar films escape with an almost clean chit. The frequent change of government policies and approaches poses one of the basic dilemmas, since films take a long time to make. Restrictions on drinking and violence and attitudes towards neighbouring countries are concrete examples. In the heat of border wars, film makers are called upon to be patriotic and make morale-boosting films. While the films are being made, peace treaties are signed and producers are told not to harm relations with friendly countries. The degree to which violence, sex or drinking is permitted also keeps changing.

Censorship, being arbitrary and inequitable, is exemplified best in the treatment of the screen kiss. It used to occur frequently in the silent and early talkie films. Then the rising spirit of nationalism and the call to avoid alien customs led to the producers voluntarily banning kissing scenes. There was never anything specific in the censorship code against the kiss and it continued to be so, but the censor turned it into an unwritten rule and exercised it when film makers later wanted it. The argument was that Indians do not kiss in public. Kisses were, however, freely allowed in imported films which the same audience saw. The illogical logic was extended to permit kisses in Indian films, provided the osculating exercise was between two non-Indian characters or if an Indian kissed a 'foreigner' (for example, a Portuguese girl in one film

above
The kiss was allowed by the censors in *Satyam Shivam Sundaram.*

right
Waheeda Rehman in a dance in the Holi ritual.

opposite
A romantic bedroom scene—the grapes are used to invite closeness and a kiss.

above
Although monster films have been banned there was no objection to scenes of gruesome violence in *Do Jhooth.*

above right
Shaitaan included scenes of rape and murder but was passed by the censor.

right
Slaughter of a People was a short feature film. Its subject was the havoc in Bangladesh at the time of Independence.

even though she was acted by an Indian). Perhaps it would have been more absurd to fight for the kiss in a court of law, as I. S. Johar wanted to try. But recent liberalising of censor attitudes has suddenly permitted the kiss in Raj Kapoor's *Satyam Shivam Sundaram.* Ironically, the industry are themselves cool about the kiss, especially the heroines.

As a reverse measure, the censor's axe has recently come down on horror instead of on realistic violence. So *Jadu Tona* and *Jaani Dushman* have been banned, though their 'monsters' would look like a fantasy even to children.

A censored scene from I. S. Johar's *Five Rifles*.

Of the sex-education films kept under a long ban after wide release, one has been passed and is being screened, though it is little different from the others. Political films have seldom been made and so questions about their censorship did not arise until the Emergency. Apart from *Kissa Kursi Ka* already discussed, regional films like *Wild Wind* in Kannada and *Rajan Paranja Katha* (the tale of the student Rajan who is alleged to have died in jail) faced very heavy weather.

The censor-producer clash occurs mainly in formulas and clichés. The usual solution is to approve devious and dubious methods of smuggling in taboo material rather than show it directly. For instance, the hero and the heroine may dash against each other or roll down together. If their packages get exchanged, he invariably opens hers and then holds up her bra screaming. If he is disguised as a woman, an old man or a fake doctor, he can take more liberties with her. A lot is also implied in the songs-dances, like the cabaret, the Indian 'mujra', the Holi revelry of sprinkling coloured water and powder, the tribal hocus-pocus in scanty dresses, the scene in the rain or the river when the heroine's dress sticks to the body and the large quantities of lyrical erotica such as songs about 'pardah' (veil) obviously standing for virginity. Bridal night sequences, bedroom acrobatics and rape attempts resembling choreographed fights are all hot favourites and considered 'legitimate' by censors.

The official role of the central government has extended to appointing several inquiry committees, the two most prominent ones being in 1927 (under British rule) and 1951. Some of the latter's recommendations were accepted and took the form of developmental and promotional bodies or schemes. Not all of them have helped the progress of cinema and the industry habitually calls them a burden. Still, a lot of good work has surely been done, which left to the laws of demand and supply in the market jungle may not have been possible at all.

Annual National Awards decided by an independent jury and given away by the President of India have acted as a big incentive to the making of better films and the selection of weightier themes. The awards, begun in 1953, are now given in several categories and for all the different languages. Many State governments have also instituted awards for their respective language films. Festivals of these films are

overleaf top left
Ashani Sanket was Satyajit Ray's film on the Bengal famine with Soumitra Chatterji as the priest facing slow degradation.

overleaf bottom left
Jai Baba Felunath was a Bengali adventure story by Ray about a detective named Feluda.

overleaf top right
Parshuram was directed by Mrinal Sen and dealt with life in the slums.

overleaf bottom right
Shabana Azmi attempts to seduce Sanjeev Kumar away from his obsession for chess in *Shatranj Ke Khiladi*.

This love scene from *Do Gaz Zameen Ke Neeche* was passed by the censors.

Umbrella is a cartoon about family planning. It was produced by the Films Division.

held in Delhi and other places and international film festivals are also organised by the Information and Broadcasting Ministry — the competitive ones in Delhi every two years and other expositions in other cities in the alternate years. These have helped to bring the world's most remarkable films to India, though briefly, since they are not regularly imported. Of course, the avid cinegoer's craze is for a feast of uncensored films for a fortnight and this is also the motivating factor behind much of the membership of film societies, now found in a fairly large number in different centres.

The government has set up the Film and TV Institute of India in Poona for training new talent. After some years of good unpublicised work the Institute entered the limelight when some of its gifted acting trainees turned into big stars. This has led to a prolonged dispute over whether the teaching courses should specialise or have a general orientation. The catch is that the Institute has produced actors and technicians but few noteworthy film makers. Also situated in Poona is the National Film Archive of India. It has made a worthy effort in salvaging and preserving films yet keeps pace with the proverbial snail in study and research, maintaining records and bringing out publications. The danger is that the Archive may become a dumping ground rather than an academic centre.

Another promotional body backed by the government is the Film Finance Corporation. After years of aimlessness the F.F.C. found its moorings with Mr. B. K. Karanjia as its chairman. Starting with Mrinal Sen's *Bhuvan Shome*, 1969, it funded a group of many Hindi and some regional films which collectively went to form what is known as the 'new cinema' movement in India composed of low budget, off-beat films. Some did go into extremes of abstraction and experimentation, without the time or the audience being ripe for them, but by and large, a new breeze had blown, if not exactly a new wave. The good work has been kept up with Mr. Jagdish Parikh, a management expert, becoming the chairman of the F.F.C. More off-beat films are being funded along with other related activities such as setting up a distribution circuit, helping to construct small art theatres, tapping the non-theatrical outlets and importing some popular films with a view to plough the profits into a better kind of Indian Cinema. The film industry complains that the organisation thrives on a commission it charges on raw stock supplied and the 'new cinema' people grumble about the collateral security being demanded against loans.

The regular trade is also critical of other bodies; the Indian Motion Pictures Export Corporation (I.M.P.E.C.) had a chequered history with its past chairmen exporting themselves around the world rather than the films. Private exporters claim that their foreign exchange earnings are much better and the I.M.P.E.C's cannelising is only a superfluous

overleaf top left
A moment of contemplation in the Malayalam film *Kanchana Sita.*

overleaf bottom left
Saudagar had Amitabh Bachchan in love with Padma Khanna (right), but married to a rich middle-aged woman.

overleaf opposite
Shabana Azmi (right) and Anant Nag in *Ankur* which was directed by Shyam Benegal.

A scene from the 1957 award-winning children's film titled *Hum Panchhi Ek Daal Ke.*

hindrance. The ministry has recently thought of disbanding it and setting up a broad based National Film Development Corporation to take many of these organisations under one wing.

The industry also expresses its dissatisfaction with the working of another old undertaking — the Hindustan Photo Films, a factory at Ooty to manufacture raw stock, which does not provide enough to meet the demand. Colour stock being yet a remote dream, the H.P.F's black and white stock has also not been found satisfactory by film makers and technicians. In any case, colour is all the vogue in all Hindi and even the better budgeted regional films, creative directors are increasingly taking to colour to ensure better results and markets.

Another organisation which has wasted itself and a lot of funds into the bargain is the Children's Film Society. After several years, it has failed to create anything like a children's film movement and the products made or imported by it rotate in a small, little-known groove. A majority of the country's children are outside its orbit and are therefore exposed to the type of feature film to which their elders are addicted. A few of the C.F.S. films have attained some measure of quality and a few awards, yet the private sector's results in this, too, are superior. Satyajit Ray, V. Shantaram and others have come up with excellent children's films.

The biggest film making unit of the government is the Films Division which has almost complete control over the making and release of documentaries and newsreels. This 'monopoly' has been a subject of much comment, though it must be said in fairness to the authorities that

The theme of Hindu-Muslim harmony was returned to in 1960 in *Idd Mubarak*, a production by the Children's Film Society.

Jaise Ko Taisa, 1966, was another highly-praised cartoon by the Children's Film Society.

without such an official backing the short-film movement would have been swept out of existence by the regular trade channels on the simple grounds that there is no profit margin. In fact, ambitious attempts of this type were nipped in the bud (like J. B. H. Wadia's *Cultural variety shorts* on some of the great performing artists made during the early 1940s). During the Second World War, the then government set up a Film Advisory Board with Mr. Wadia as the chairman. After Independence, when all short film making units were defunct, the Indian government started the Films Division in 1948.

Since then, it has made hundreds of shorts of various types which have the privilege of 22 minutes' compulsory screening all over India and even earning a small rental from the theatres. The Division also covers independent documentary makers by allotting them films or approving purchase through a committee. Another advantage is the nurture of talents which could then branch off into other fields. Feature films can be enriched by those from the documentary field. Somewhat similar is the case of radio and television, until now run by the government and on the point of being made autonomous. The commercial section of All India Radio banks almost wholly on film songs and sponsored film programmes. Its huge earnings are justified only because formerly it used to be pocketed by the commercial service of Radio Ceylon. The 10 or so T.V. centres which have come up during the 1970s also have feature films, song extracts from them or appearance of film personalities as the most viewed programmes. Rather than T.V. shaking up the movie industry, as in other countries, it is T.V. which has become movie-subjugated. Such is the power of the Indian feature film.

All the aid and developmental efforts have not succeeded in improving standards except on a peripheral level. The film industry laments being the most taxed film industry in the world. It is taxed on various levels from raw stock to final print. The biggest chunk is collected by the different state governments as entertainment tax, the total going above a staggering 100 crores per year. When the question of aid comes, the buck is passed between the two levels of government, state and central. The argument for non-intervention in the private sector applies mainly to the type of films and the kind of people who enter the field to make them. It is a moot point whether so much tax revenue would accrue if the films were not so escapist and commercially orientated. Perhaps, the public exchequer, too, has a stake in poor quality.

Rays of Hope

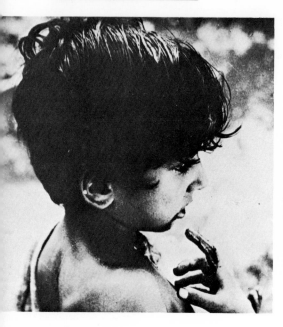

above
Subir Bannerjee as Apu in *Pather Panchali*.

opposite top
Sharmila Tagore in *Apur Sansar*.

opposite below
A scene from Satyajit Ray's full-length documentary *Rabindranath Tagore* which won the President's Gold Medal.

When we look at the whole of Indian Cinema a sense of despondency is bound to descend. 13,560 films in different languages were made from 1931 to 1978 and 500-600 are now being made each year, but with little aim or purpose.

Somehow, the dark cloud does have some silver linings. There are a few rays of hope that the medium will be used in the way it was intended — for artistic expression, thematic thrust, cinematic exploration and communication mixed with sensible entertainment. The film maker who raised such hopes for the first time, initiating a whole new type of film with little link to the Indian film's past is Satyajit Ray. Arriving in 1955 with *Pather Panchali* (Saga of the Road), Ray has kept fulfilling the high hopes he raised with a series of important films, which have won endless appreciation abroad as indicated by some of the world's major awards and honours. His path-finding has become a source of inspiration for the avant-garde film movement, mainly in regional languages but also in Hindi.

A detailed discussion of all of Ray's works would need a separate book. Still, to summarise them within the compass of this book, Ray has made 25 films (counting *Teen Kanya* as three self-contained films) and five documentaries. His films started on a level which had not been touched till then and, whether we like it or not, they are still unmatched. Though the works of several other film makers have been exported and given a wide exposure through festivals and other means, they have not been able to compare in awards or approbation.

Ray's early struggles to make his first film were almost akin to those of pioneer Phalke. Finally, the West Begal government took an unprecedented step of becoming a film producer for *Pather Panchali*. With *Aparajito* (The Unvanquished) and *Apur Sansar* (The World of Apu) it forms a trilogy that has carved its own unique niche in world cinema. Ray himself describes its theme as the growth of a person from childhood to manhood and his final acceptance of life and its responsibility.

Before making the third part of the Apu trilogy in 1959, Ray made films in two totally contrasted genres: a social fantasy and a study of feudal decline. The first was *Parash Pathar* (The Philosopher's Stone), a serio-comic look at an aged clerk who finds a stone that can turn anything into gold. *Jalsaghar* (The Music Room) was a sad, lingering look at a landlord who slowly goes down into the dust, hanging desperately to the last threads of his former glory while his neighbour, a parvenu, enriches himself through commerce and supercedes him.

In 1960, Ray's *Devi* (The Goddess) made a foray in a new direction — religious dogmatism and blind beliefs of divine incarnation in mortal form, which destroy the life of an ordinary human being. In the Tagore birth centenary year, Ray's tributes took the form of a full-length documentary, his first, called *Rabindranath Tagore* (also made in a shorter version). But his own creative interpretation of Tagore was *Teen Kanya* from three stories revolving round three typical females at different stages of life. The whole concept became bulky, so only two films were sent abroad as *Two Daughters*, leading to many a curious

inquiry about 'where is the third daughter?' Ray's supreme vision turned *Postmaster* into a haunting tale of a little village orphan who has a brief encounter with kindness and affection, *Monihara* into a thrilling study of a woman with a morbid infatuation for jewellery and *Samaapti* (The Conclusion) into a hilarious account of a tomboy reaching puberty and accepting her husband.

Filming *Kanchanjungha* in colour, Ray took a new direction in studying a set of wealthy unhappy people dominated by a materialistic family head. In contrast, the next was *Abhijaan* about a Rajput descendant reduced to the level of a cab driver but living up to his heredity in the relationships he finally strikes with people.

Then came two major achievements in quick succession: *Mahanagar* (The Big City) and *Charulata* (The Lonely Woman). The former was a deep and realistic insight into a middle class family and a typical Bengali housewife's attempt to take up a job with all the repercussions this causes. *Charulata*, an acknowledged masterpiece, was Tagore's tale about a neglected wife and her attachment to her husband's cousin, given a superbly different cinematic entity. Both films brought a fresh surge of acclaim and awards for Ray.

The twin film *Kapurush-O-Mahapurush* (The Coward and The Holy Man) was a two-in-one humorous look at the foibles of man. The first had a cowardly lover who ditches his girl and meets her again after she is

above
Samapti was adapted from a Tagore story of a tomboy who is married prematurely. Aparna Das Gupta was the heroine.

right
Madhabi Mukherjee as the neglected wife in Satyajit Ray's Bengali film *Charulata*.

married to a rich man. The beauty of the film lay in a double-edged interpretation left open for the audience — did the husband know everything about the former love affair and was playing a game in collaboration with his wife or was he unaware of what was happening? The second film exposed the hoaxy world of Indian 'babas' and 'swamis', who thrive on the anxiety of the poor to become rich and the rich to relieve their consciences.

Robi Ghosh and Topen Chatterji in
Goupi Gyne and Bagha Byne.

A scene from *Seemabaddha*, 1971.

Nayak (The Hero) was an unmasking of a movie idol. By highlighting the pitfalls of his tinsel world and pitting a woman reporter against him, Ray showed the hollowness of the star system in the box-office cinema. A weak spot in Ray's career came with *Chidiyakhana*, a detective thriller he did not want to do. In *Gopi Gyne and Bagha Byne* (Adventures of Gopi and Bagha) he again showed his mastery over a new genre, a musical fantasy for children, but not without a subtle undercurrent of political metaphor, about two neighbouring kingdoms ruled by two brothers seeking peace from war.

Satyajit Ray and Sharmila Tagore on the set of *Aranyer Din Raatri.*

Aranyer Din Raatri (Days and Nights in the Forest) was, like *Kanchanjungha*, an intimate look at urban people and their complex entanglements during a sojourn in the forest. Then a new trilogy about contemporary and youth problems, set in Calcutta, took shape with *Pratidwandi* (Siddhartha and the city) about unemployment and the destruction of values. This was followed by *Seemabaddha* (Company Ltd.) about employed people in the ratrace, stooping to any tactics in their climb to the top. The third and most hard-hitting was *Jana Aranya* (The Middleman) about an unemployed Bengali youth taking to business and ending up by having to pimp for his own friend's sister.

Before the third film, there were again two in other genres. *Sonar Kella* (The Golden Fortress) was an enjoyable detective film for children and

was sponsored by the West Bengal government. *Ashani Sanket* (Distant Thunder) was set in the period just preceding the outbreak of the Bengal famine and the corrosion of human values which it sets off. After this Ray finally stepped into the world of Hindi cinema but on his own terms. *Shatranj Ke Khiladi* (The Chess Players), discussed elsewhere in this book, sparked off controversies, distribution disputes and so on, with the usual conclusion — acclaim abroad but a lukewarm reception in India.

Ray has also filmed *Joi Baba Felunath* in Bengali, another adventure cum mystery. His short documentaries include *Two* made for the Esso World Theatre, a wordless film about a rich and a poor boy; *Sikkim* about the mountain Kingdom, although Ray was unhappy with the result. *The Inner Eye* on a blind painter of Shantiniketan who was once his teacher and *Bala* on the famous Natyam dancer.

The 'new cinema' movement from 1968 till today has taken various forms. Hindi film makers have usually been too bogged down by their economic problems to make a real breakthrough except in bilinguals tagged on to essentially regional films. Since Hindi is the all-India language it is said to be lacking provincial roots, though this is not completely true. The real problem lies in making the Hindi art film acceptable to the different states, its own language zones being indifferent to this kind of effort. Yet, following Mrinal Sen's *Bhuvan Shome* there have been some good, off-beat efforts. Basu Chatterji, who started with the F.F.C. — aided *Sara Akash* (The entire sky) about a new bride of an unwilling groom, made *Rajnigandha* (Flowers). Though a simple romantic dilemma, of a woman tossed between two lovers, it was done in a totally fresh style with new artists and spot shooting and achieved heartening success. Basu followed it up with *Chhoti Si Baat* (Just a word) and *Chit Chor* (The thief of the heart), while his *Swami*, based on Sarat Chandra, was in the Bengali mould — simple and serious. His films travel the regular commercial circuit and seem a meeting ground between the art film and the formula one.

Basu Bhattacharya is another who has consistently made unusual films, using stars and a few songs. After *Teesri Kasam*, a folk musical in the Bihar province, and the experimental *Uski Kahani* (His story), he made a trilogy on marital maladjustment (already discussed) and tackled other subjects in *Tumhara Kalloo* (Yours Kalloo), *Daaku* (Dacoit) and *Sangat* (Company), giving them a fresh outlook.

Gulzar is another who makes superior films in a popular format like his mentor Hrishikesh Mukherji, who also comes from the Bimal Roy camp. His films *Achanak* (Sudden), *Koshish* (Attempt), *Mere Apne* (Our own people), *Mausam* (Season) and the political *Aandhi* (Storm) have earned him a good reputation as an interesting and clever director. These directors seldom seek loans from the F.F.C., as they manage to raise finance from the trade, on the strength of their own names as well as those of the few stars who work with them for prestige.

A stormy petrel is B. R. Ishara, who arrived with *Chetna* (already discussed) but then was derailed with several films which were failures. His films have a rather rough and crude approach and his exposure of the female anatomy usually gets him into trouble with censors, while his firebrand themes create difficulties with distributors. Many of his films are unreleased even after their ban is lifted.

Shyam Benegal is the Hindi film maker who has best maintained the balance between unusualness and acceptability at the box-office. After a career in advertising films and some documentaries, his first feature *Ankur* (The Seedling) received critical acclaim with its treatment of a young landlord's exploitation of a pretty maid servant married to a handicapped man. It introduced highly talented artists, Shabana Azmi (who also became a star in the popular cinema), Anant Nag and Sadhu Meher. Benegal's following films were *Nishant* (End of the night) on a helpless man's wife abducted by powerful zamindars culminating in mass violence, *Manthan* (The churning) on the teething troubles of a co-operative society movement for a milk scheme (actually financed by members of one such society in Saurashtra), *Bhumika* (The Role) inspired from the life of a permissive but unhappy actress and *Kondura* (name) on a boon which becomes a curse. (The last one is a Telugu-Hindi bilingual.) This was followed by *Junoon* (Wrath) for star Shashi Kapoor, a romantic tale set during the Indian Mutiny in 1857.

Among other attempts to combine quality with box-office safety were Ved Rahi's *Daraar* on the fear psychosis caused by war and *Prem Parbat* on a young woman's suppressed urges while being married to an old impotent man. Producer Tarachand Barjatya, who has a huge distribution-exhibition network, has also promoted as his own productions some typically Indian and likable films including *Geet Gaata Chal* (Sing on) inspired from Tagore and directed by Hiren Nag and *Saudagar* (Merchant) directed by Sudhendu Roy about a Muslim jaggery-maker who weds and divorces a middle-aged woman, only to earn the money to marry an attractive girl.

Kantilal Rathod, again coming from the field of documentary and animation films, made a remarkable Gujarati film *Kanku* (name) with F.F.C. loan about a bold peasant widow, who slips just once with the village money-lender, but whose marriage is arranged by the villagers with a bumpkin. After another film *Parinay* (Marriage) on an ill-matched couple, Rathod began *Ramnagari* (The world of Ram) based on the autobiography of a barber who wanted to rise higher. H. K. Verma's *Kadambari* (name), R. N. Shukla's *Mrig Trishna* (Mirage), Vikas and Aruna's *Shaque* (Doubt), Bhim Sain's *Gharaonda* (Nest) have been other notable films produced independently.

From the F.F.C. group M. S. Sathyu's *Garm Hawa* (Hot winds) took up a very topical but touchy theme about the isolation felt by the Muslim community in India in the face of the eternal attraction for Pakistan, through the story of an unlucky family which finally realises that its roots lie in India and its fate is the same as that of the other Indian masses. But Sathyu's second *Kanneshwar Rama* (about a legendary dacoit) made in Kannada-Hindi could not hold a candle to the brilliance of the first film. Avtar Kaul, who died prematurely, left *27 Down* as his first and last film about an average youth cowed down by parental pressure into accepting a mundane loveless existence. The film, a flop at first, became fairly successful five years after its making. Raakhee, the only star in the film, had by then become a popular and much publicised figure.

In 1969 Basu Chatterji directed *Sara Akash*, a sensitive depiction of the problems of a new bride. This was one of the films backed by the Film Finance Corporation.

The Hindi director Shyam Benegal (seated).

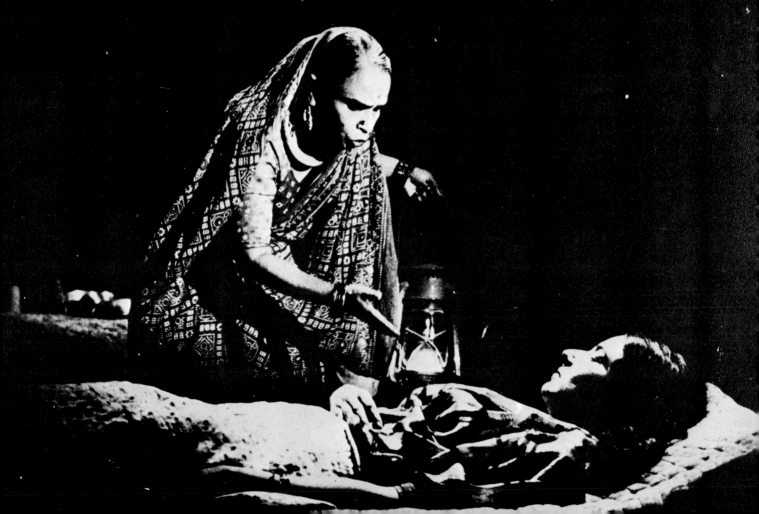

The F.F.C. has, of course, also had failures including Mani Kaul's formalistic *Uski Roti* (His bread), *Ashadh Ka Ek Din* (A day in the month of Ashadh) and *Duvidha* (Dilemma) which could not find regular release. This also happened with Kumar Shahani's *Maya Darpan* (Illusion) and also Raj Marbros' *Trisandhya* (Twilight) made in Malayalam-Hindi with star Waheeda Rehman. Films released with little success were Girish Vaidya's *Aakrant* (Encircled), M. Prabhat's *Grahan* (Eclipse) and Girish Ranjan's *Dak Bangla* (Rest house). New films made with the F.F.C. include Yukt Cooperative's two films *Ghashiram Kotwal* (Name) and *Arvind Desai Ki Ajeeb Dastaan* (The strange case of Arvind Desai), M. Saral's *Tyaag Patra* (Resignation), Rajinder Singh Bedi's *Aankhin Dekhi* (Eye-witnessed) and Muzaffar Ali's *Gaman* (Transition).

Mrinal Sen has been the most consistent and prolific regional director and has also made the Hindi films *Ek Adhuri Kahani* (An incomplete story) and *Mrigayaa* (The Royal Hunt) as well as forays into other tongues like the Oriya with *Matira Manisha* (Man of the soil) and the Telugu with *Oka Oorie Katha* (A village tale) based on Premchand's story *Kafan* (The shroud). But his forte is naturally his home-based work in Bengali. Even before *Bhuvan Shome* he had made outstanding art films in Bengali. His later body of work include *Interview, Calcutta '71, Padatik, Chorus* and *Parshuram.*

The late Ritwick Ghatak, talented but erratic, made some notable Bengali films: *Suvarnarekha, Meghe Dhake Tara, Jukti Takko Ar Gappo.* Other creative directors include Purnendu Patrea, Tapan Sinha, Rajen Tarafdar and Tarun Majumdar. The Bengali film, always in the vanguard faced a sad decline a few years ago and has still to recover. As if to fill the void, an unexpected resurgence has come from the South, lost for a long time in mass production of purely box-office films.

But in the last five years, all the four languages have sprung surprises. Malayalam led the movement, with Adoor Gopalakrishnan making the award-winners *Swayamvaram* and *Kodeyettom*, and others producing *Nirmalyam, Swapnam, Chattkari, Nellu, Dweep, Uttarayanam, Swapnadanam, Mohiniyettam, Chuvana Vithukal, Agni* and *Kanchana Seetha*. In Tamil, progress has been slow (with 'new wave' still a dreaded word), seen in a few films like *Dikkatra Parvati, Dhakom, Agraharthil Kazhutai* (Donkey In a Brahmin Quarter).

In Kannada, *Samskara*, (first banned and then awarded the President's Gold Medal), was the first of several anti-Brahminist films which also trickled into other languages. Girish Karnad's *Kaadu, Tabbaliyu Nenade Magane* ('Go-Dhuli' in Hindi) and *Ondanondu Kalladali* have also made a mark, apart from many others including *Vamsha Vriksha, Chomana Dudi, Hamsa Geethe, Kokila, Karavali, Pallavi, Anuroopa, Rishya Shringa* and 1978's major award-winner *Ghatashraddha* by Girish Kasaravalli.

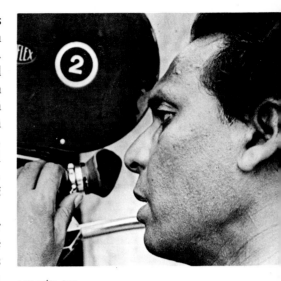

opposite top
Mrinal Sen's Hindi film *Mrigayaa* (The Royal Hunt), 1976, with Mamta Shankar (left) and Mithun Chakravarty.

opposite bottom
Kanku was acclaimed as the best Gujarati film of 1969 and is considered one of the first of the 'new wave' of films.

above
Mrinal Sen

Swayamvaram, a Malayalam film directed by Adoor Gopalkrishnan.

opposite
A scene from the Tamil film
Agraharathil Kazhutai (Donkey in a
Brahmin Quarter).

above
Chomana Dudi was a film in Kannada
about an untouchable portrayed by
Vasudeo Rao.

left
Another 'new wave' film in Kannada
was *Samskara*, which had an anti-
Brahmin theme.

In other languages, the Oriya *Kanaklata* and *Chhilka Teerey*, the
Assamese *Sandhya Raag* and *Chameli Memsaab*, the Marathi *Shantata
Court Chalu Ahe, Saamna, Jait Re Jait*, the Gujarati *Kanku* and *Janamteep*
hold out the high hope that the future of the better and truer Indian
Cinema may lie with the regional film. In any case, they will have to be
films made with integrity, competence, vision and dedication. Then
India will not only be just the largest film-producing country in the
world but also one of the better film-producing countries, whose films
the world looks forward to seeing.

Index

Page numbers in bold type refer to illustrations. Each Indian name has been indexed by its first word except for those names that are preceded by initials, which have been indexed under their first full names. Western names are listed by surname. For example, Jaya Bhaduri is indexed under Jaya, J. F. Madan is indexed under Madan and Jennifer Kendal is listed under Kendal. Some film titles have been followed in brackets by their nearest possible translations; these are neither official titles nor alternative ones unless specifically mentioned and so have not been indexed.